The Geneva Accord

Other books by Rabbi Michael Lerner

Healing Israel/Palestine:
A Path to Reconciliation and Peace

Jewish Renewal:
A Path to Healing and Transformation

The Politics of Meaning:
Restoring Hope and Possibility in an Age of Cynicism

The Socialism of Fools:
Anti-Semitism on the Left

Spirit Matters:
Global Healing and the Wisdom of the Soul

Surplus Powerlessness:
The Psychodynamics of Everyday Life and the
Psychology of Individual and Social Transformation

Jews & Blacks:
A Dialogue on Race, Religion, and Culture in America
(with Cornel West)

The Geneva Accord

And Other Strategies for Healing the Israeli-Palestinian Conflict

Rabbi Michael Lerner

THE TERRA NOVA SERIES

North Atlantic Books

Berkeley • California

Published by
North Atlantic Books
P.O. Box 12327   Cover and book design by
Berkeley, California 94712   Paula Morrison

Printed in the United States of America
Distributed to the book trade by Publishers Group West

The Geneva Accord: And Other Strategies for Healing the Israeli-Palestinian Conflict is sponsored by the Society for the Study of Native Arts and Sciences, a nonprofit educational corporation whose goals are to develop an educational and crosscultural perspective linking various scientific, social, and artistic fields; to nurture a holistic view of arts, sciences, humanities, and healing; and to publish and distribute literature on the relationship of mind, body, and nature.

Library of Congress Cataloging-in-Publication Data
Lerner, Michael.
  The Geneva accord : and other strategies for healing the
Israeli-Palestinian conflict / by Michael Lerner.
    p. cm. — (The Terra Nova Series)
  ISBN 1-55643-537-1 (pbk.)
  1. Arab-Israeli conflict—1993—Peace. 2. Peace building—Middle East.
I. Title. II. Series.
DS119.76.L468 2004
954.05'3—dc22

                                   2004006212

1 2 3 4 5 6 7 8 9 DATA 09 08 07 06 05 04

Contents

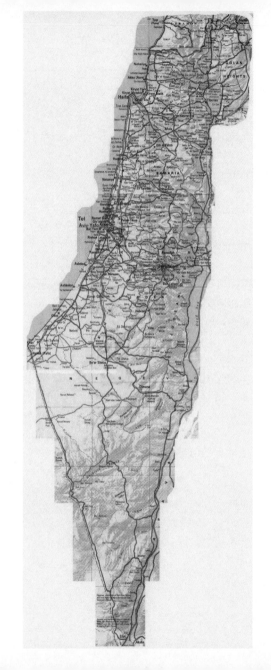

Introduction

The conflict between Israel and Palestine can end. It is not a reflection of some eternal struggle that can never be solved. It is not the product of hatreds that are so intractable that they will always defeat the best intentions of the good-hearted. And when it is solved, people will look back and wonder why the obvious steps to a solution were not taken sooner and more decisively.

A major step forward, in fact, was taken in December 2003, when key figures in Israel and Palestine met in Switzerland to celebrate the release of the Geneva Accord—a detailed agreement that specifies possible terms of a resolution that would be acceptable to mainstream elements in both societies. Yet the Geneva Accord has not been embraced by Israel or by its primary political ally in the world, the United States. Why give it so much attention? Because for the first time since the creation of the State of Israel we have the detailed forerunner of an agreement that could actually work if there were the political will to implement it.

In this short book, I'll show you what is so exciting about the Geneva Accord, what its limitations are, and what the alternative strategies are for achieving Middle East peace. I'll consider the critical arguments that have been brought against the Geneva Accord from both those who complain that the

Accord "gives too much to the Palestinians" and those who believe that it is merely a clever Zionist ploy to maintain Jewish control and domination of its Arab minority.

In my previous book, *Healing Israel/Palestine* (North Atlantic Books, 2003), I presented a detailed history of the Arab-Israeli conflict from a perspective that is rarely heard: I showed how both sides have legitimate claims, how both sides have been remarkably insensitive and cruel to the other, and how both sides have contributed to digging the current predicament/mess. It is my contention that a solution to the struggle between Israel and Palestine requires abandoning a discourse of "blaming the Other" and of seeking to portray one side (whichever one you choose) as "the righteous victim" and the other as "the hateful and destructive Other." Both sides bear considerable moral responsibility for past actions, and both sides need a significant change of approach to the other. It is because the Geneva Accord is a concrete and significant step in that direction that it deserves our attention, even if there are no immediate signs that the relevant governments are ready to seriously embrace it.

Yet, as I will also make clear, there are deficiencies in the Accord; it is certainly not the only possible strategy to end the Occupation. I will consider other strategies for peace currently being discussed by peace forces in both communities.

1. The Historical Background

Jews did not return to their ancient homeland to oppress another people and Palestinians did not oppose their return because of some pre-existing hatred of Jews. Both peoples had a history within which they interpreted and managed to systematically misunderstand the intentions and motives of the other.

The Palestinian perception that the Jews intended to displace them was nurtured in part by ruling elites in the Arab world who feared that the imposition of Western capitalist and socialist ideas in their area would destabilize their feudal societies and excite Arab unrest. Those elites, often acting through their surrogates who ran the local mosques, did all they could to inflame anti-Jewish sentiments in the twentieth century and to convince the Arabs and their often-uneducated masses that the Jews were intent on expelling all Arabs.

From the standpoint of many Arabs, the Jews were coming to Palestine as surrogates for Western colonialism. And—there was nothing fanciful in their perception that the European powers were committed to domination of the Middle East and that their championing of Jewish immigration was in part to advance European colonial interests.

Scattered around the globe, Jews were unified by a religious tradition whose daily prayers called for their return to an ancient homeland from which they had been forcibly expelled by Roman imperialism; they also called for the rebuilding of the ancient Temple in Jerusalem and the re-creation of Jewish cultural life. The vast majority of Jews who came to Palestine between 1880 and 1930 were eco-nomically impoverished refugees from Eastern Europe who had voyaged there in the belief that their safety could only be achieved in a land where Jews had control over their own institutions.

Acts of hostility toward them by indigenous Arabs did not surprise refugees returning from generations of embattled exile. Ever since they had been forced into the Diaspora from their holy land, Jews had had to confront local populations who treated them with disdain often erupting into anger and violence. In fact, it was precisely the millennia-long history of what appeared to Jews to be unprovoked hostility from non-Jews that gave plausibility to the Zionist argument that Jews needed a state and an army of their own to defend themselves. The Arab notion that they were somehow agents of colonialism or "Europeans" seemed ludicrous to most Jewish settlers, who knew that they themselves had been a primary victim of European imperialism for the past eight-een hundred years as well as the single group most demeaned and oppressed by Christian societies and their secular successors.

When the Jewish settlement in Palestine ("the Yishuv") encountered violent resistance to its expansion, Jews interpreted this not as anti-imperialism but as an extension of the predictable anti-Semitism that had permeated the cultures of non-Jews everywhere throughout most of Jewish history. All the more reason, they thought, to build Jewish institutions that would protect them.

Conversely, the creation of Jewish-only institutions in the Yishuv seemed a confirmation of the worst fears of the Palestinians, particularly when Jewish communities began to flourish. (They were financed in part by Jews in the West who adopted the Zionist enterprise as an insurance policy against future flare-ups of anti-Semitism.) When the Jewish labor movement subsequently convinced Jewish capitalist enterprises to hire "Jewish labor" to the exclusion of the Arabs (even when the latter would work for less money), and when Jews began to build whole new cities and to train a domestic army to protect their settlements, Arabs drew the obvious conclusion that these outsiders were slowly building the foundation for a society whose aim was to replace them. The idealized Jewish homeland was being constructed atop a living culture as if Arab buildings and orchards were no more than archeological ruins.

Palestinian Arabs began to use their influence with the surrounding Arab states to pressure England to cut off immigration to Palestine in the 1930s and 1940s. Fearful of a severing of Arab oil supplies that were needed to fight Nazism, the English complied. Key leaders of the Palestinian world forged open alliances with the Nazis and, as Jews sat in refugee camps, did all they could to prevent them from coming to Palestine.

Outrage at the moral bankruptcy of policies pursued by the Palestinian national movement and its successful alliance with the British against Jewish immigration finally led Jews to launch a full-scale struggle against British colonialism— a struggle which soon became a civil war between Jews and Palestinians. That war escalated dramatically when the British announced their intentions to give up their Mandate over Palestine. Surrounding Arab states then declared war on the newly proclaimed State of Israel.

The Palestinians rejected the United Nations' offer of a partition of Palestine in 1947 which would have given them approximately forty-eight percent of the land. By the end of the war, which lasted from 1947–49, the Palestinians were left instead with approximately twenty-two percent of pre-1948 Palestine, and that part was occupied by Jordan (the West Bank) and Egypt (the Gaza strip). So while Jews celebrated the War of Independence as a modern miracle, Palestinians memorialized it as Al Nakba, the Great Disaster.

The scope of the Great Disaster for the Palestinians was

measured by somewhere between 700,000 and 800,000 Palestinian civilians having fled their homes in the struggle, most of them to protect their families from acts of violence by Jewish terrorist groups led by future Israeli Prime Ministers Menachem Begin and Yitzhak Shamir. When Israel refused to allow these Palestinians to return to their homes after the hostilities had ended, this huge civilian population became homeless and nationless, the original Palestinian refugees.

First under the leadership of Yasser Arafat and the Palestinian Liberation Organization, later (when the PLO became more moderate and repudiated terror in favor of a negotiated settlement with Israel) under the leadership of Islamic groups like Hamas and Islamic Jihad, Palestinians came to believe with more and more certainty that the best strategy to regain their lands was to terrorize Israeli civilians until they tired of the fight. Lacking an army that could meet the Israeli military in the field of battle, Palestinian refugees chose the tools of violence and fear that had become increasingly popular among other national liberation struggles resisting colonial oppressions.

Only the circumstances here were very difficult. Israelis were not a group of settlers who might choose to return to the homeland that had sponsored them, for instance, in the way that French settlers in Algeria might someday return to France. They had no alternative but to build a safe society where they were—as the State of Israel. Terrorist tactics might enrage and even frighten them, but there was no chance it would drive them out. On the contrary, terrorism convinced the Jews that they had no alternative but to protect themselves against a fundamentally hostile Palestinian population. And this meant an even stronger military.

In 1967 Egypt demanded that the United Nations remove an international security force it had placed between Israel and Egypt. The soldiers were there to provide a safety barrier between the embattled sides. Egyptian leader Gamal Nasser threatened to invade Israel and, in his swaggering words, push the Israelis into the sea. Syria allied itself with Egypt, putting their own might behind Nasser's threats. Israel took preemptive action by invading Egypt and Syria. Though Israel frantically appealed to Jordan to stay out of the battle, King Hussein felt compelled to join his Arab brothers and sisters and so opened another front in the Jordanian-occupied West Bank. Thus, Israel's lightning victory in the Six Day War left it in the position of occupying both Gaza and the West Bank and thereby ruling over several million Arabs.

From the start of this Occupation, many Israelis warned against holding these conquered territories, arguing that the attempt to wield influence over and control Palestinians would weaken Israel both militarily and morally. But as long as the most serious opposition to the Occupation took the form of acts of terror by the Palestinian Liberation Organization, the more expansionist and triumphalist voices prevailed in Israeli politics. Instead of immediately establishing Palestinian self-rule—something the local population had not enjoyed under Jordanian occupation either—Israel began to construct their own settlements right there in the West Bank and Gaza, colonies that would strengthen its hold over the land and make withdrawal increasingly logistically untenable, hence politically implausible. Some Jews, in fact, believed that the 1967 victory was a sign from God that the they were intended to rule over all of the ancient Land of Israel, and they began a heroic colonizing enterprise.

It didn't help matters that international opposition to the settlements first manifested in a United Nations resolution also proclaiming that "Zionism is racism." The UN had already lost considerable credibility inside Israel by its craven submission to dictator Nasser's 1967 demand for a withdrawal of a security force that was actually protecting both sides from each other. To now dismiss the entire national-liberation struggle of the Jewish people as racist was perceived by most Jews as morally outrageous. After all, nothing Jews had carried in their struggle to achieve national liberation had come close to matching the level of murder, assassinations, and exile of populations caused by the clashes between Muslim and Hindu populations in India/Pakistan 1948–1950 or the subjugation and genocide of populations by the Soviet Union and by China, to mention just a few contemporary examples.

A feeling of isolation, rooted in the real-life experience of a culture dominated by generations of Diaspora capped by a Holocaust, increasingly contributed to the credibility of those within Israel who advocated reliance on military force and the development of nuclear weapons rather than on cooperation with neighbors as the "most realistic" path for national survival. "Never again!" a slogan developed by Jews to insist that they would never submit passively to the genocidal fantasies of anti-Semites, had a shadow side, for it spoke to more than just potential anti-Semites and, like any slogan, was blind to shifting circumstance. It should *not* have meant "never again to live in peace, never again to trust neighbors, never again to empathize with those don't share our dreams but have dreams of their own that stand in our way."

Israel's capacity to resist international pressures against the Occupation increasingly depended on its special relationship with the United States. U.S. support for Israel in the first two decades of its existence was based largely on domestic political considerations. However, in the aftermath of the 1967 victory, a group of cold warriors became newly enamored of Israel's military potential; they were convinced that Israel could be relied upon as a strategic ally in the planet-wide struggle with communism. Even after communism declined as an active threat to American economic and political domination, U.S. elites continued to believe that Israel would be a useful ally and potential staging area for future global struggles. So the U.S. consistently used its veto power in the UN to ensure that the world community could not act in concert to push Israel toward an equitable accommodation with the Palestinian people, and in turn Israel became an unquestioning and loyal supporter of U.S. economic interests and political stances throughout the world and allied its military and intelligence agencies with U.S. The Israeli-American connection is now far more substantial and deeply rooted in actual strategic agendas and mutual aid than it was when it was primarily based on political and philosophical predilections.

Israel's superior economic position allowed it to survive even in the face of an economic boycott by its Arab neighbors. Yet a thriving economy hardly camouflaged a morally corrupting Occupation. The majority of Israelis remained blissfully ignorant of the suffering of the Palestinian people under Israeli control. Convinced of their own greater level of humanity and ethical standard than that of other occupying powers, proud of what they considered the higher moral standards of their citizen army, imagining themselves to be immunized from abusing other peoples by their long cultural experience of Diaspora and Holocaust, and completely unwilling therefore even to consider the claims of Palestinians to a right to return to their former homes, many mainstream Israelis slipped a collective step further into the make-believe of their own patriotic fervor; they soon found it almost impossible to imagine that there was a Palestinian people, much less a people whose rights were being denied by them. Their belief in their own piety made the existence of such a situation initially incredible, a dishonest fiction invented by their enemy, finally a dangerous blasphemy they could not utter to themselves. When their fellow Israelis, members of the peace movement that begot institutions like B'tselem, the Israeli Human Rights Organization, began to document actual human rights violations that were the daily experience of the Palestinian people, many Israelis refused to listen, preferring to believe that for some unknown reason these fellow citizens had become "self-hating Jews" or traitors or were otherwise motivated by a hatred of their own people and a willingness to fabricate lies in order to make Israel look malign.

A prolonged militant rebellion began in 1988. The Intifada was a mass uprising; its persistence made it increasingly difficult to deny the existence of a Palestinian people. Finally, by the early 1990s, and in part as a reward to the United States for its willingness to challenge one of the region's most intense haters of Israel (Saddam Hussein's Iraq), the right-wing Likud government of Yitzhak Shamir entered into negotiations in Madrid aimed at providing some solution to the Middle East struggle.

Yet simultaneously the Shamir government was accelerating the construction of West Bank settlements and crisscrossing the land with new roads that led directly to the front doors of the settlers. President George Bush senior, recognizing that U.S. interests might be better served by working out friendlier relations with the Arab countries, insisted on withholding loan guarantees to settle new Soviet Jewry refugees from Eastern Europe until the Shamir government stopped spending its money on West Bank construction.

This kind of challenge from the U.S. contributed to the willingness of Soviet Jews living in Israel to defect from their normally conservative, anti-Palestinian instincts and vote for what became the new government of Yitzhak Rabin, who promised a peace settlement with the Palestinians as well as an end to settlement activity. In turn, Rabin sent his personal emissary, Yossi Beilin, to negotiate secretly with the Palestine Liberation Organization.

The Oslo Accords of 1993 were based on the exchange of "land for peace." The formal agreement envisioned a three-stage process of Israeli withdrawal from the West Bank and Gaza, culminating in a final settlement of the conflict to be negotiated during the last stage of withdrawals—stipulated to take place within five years. Yossi Beilin explained to the Palestinian negotiators that the three-stage process was necessary to build confidence among Israelis that the Palestinians would not use the withdrawals to weaken Israeli security and unleash a new round of terrorists. Yet he also assured the negotiators that Yitzhak Rabin would support a complete withdrawal to the pre-1967 borders with "minor border modifications" to allow Israel to incorporate a few sensitive settlements into Israel proper. Palestinians would thus be in full charge and have full sovereignty over the twenty-two percent of pre-1948 Palestine that had not been absorbed by Israel.

The Oslo Accords were greeted with great expectations and hopefulness by majorities on both sides. However, also on both sides, strong minorities were convinced that the fundamental notion of a two-state solution embedded in the Oslo Accords was not only a mistake but a potential catastrophe to their interests, a resolution to be avoided at all costs. Islamic fundamentalists insisted that the real occupation was not that of 1967 but of 1948 (the founding of the State of Israel) and that the only appropriate Islamic goal should be "the liberation of all of Palestine from the Jordan to the Mediterranean." Increasingly articulating this goal within the framework of an Islamic fundamentalist worldview, these Oslo-rejectionists supported acts of terror against Israel. Conversely, many Jewish fundamentalists believed that the entire Land of Israel was willed by God to be under the dominion of the Jewish people. In the first major act of terrorist violence after the signing of Oslo, a right-wing Jewish settler named Baruch Goldstein entered the Mosque in Hebron and murdered twenty-seven Muslims at prayer.

Two sides, mirror images of each other, each backed by a God who seemed primitive, xenophobic, and warlike by modern standards of religious charity and compassion, were equally certain that divine law guaranteed them the exact same land. It never occurred to either of them that there might be a legitimate opposing interpretation—or in fact that their own position so mirrored that of their enemy. It should be no surprise that Islamic fundamentalists and Jewish fundamentalists, sworn to the death to obliterate each other, are actually allies against the majority of peace-loving Palestinians and Israelis.

Within Israel, civil strife dramatically escalated as right-wing religious groups sought to block the implementation of

13

Oslo. As civil disobedience against the Rabin government's peace policies increased, growing numbers of ultra-religious settlers and their supporters began to whisper and then, self-emboldened, holler about Rabin as a murderer and betrayer of the Jewish people. Finally one student at a prominent Jewish religious university took the law into his own hands, shooting and killing Yitzhak Rabin.

Meanwhile, the international and Israeli media talked as though the Oslo process was still happily in effect, but the daily life experience of Palestinians was that the Occupation was intensifying. When Oslo was signed, there were an estimated 150,000 settlers, whereas by the summer of 2000, when Israeli Prime Minister Ehud Barak summoned the United States and the Palestinian Authority to a Camp David Summit to propose new terms of a settlement, the number had doubled to 300,000 (instead of decreasing to zero as Oslo had seemed to promise). Moreover, during the bulk of the Rabin government's stewardship, and during the subsequent governments, conditions of daily life had grown more and more onerous for ordinary Palestinian civilians. Israel had, supposedly for "security reasons," created a network of checkpoints throughout the West Bank and Gaza, making it necessary for Palestinians to undergo humiliating body searches and hours-long waits when they sought to travel a few miles from their home towns to those of neighboring villages or towns. To support the increased population of the settlements and to insure the security of the settlers, Israel was building yet more Jewish settler-only superhighways that ran from West Bank settlements to Israel, expropriating Palestinian land.

It was no wonder, then, that Palestinians were deeply skeptical as they entered the Camp David negotiations. Israeli Prime Minister Ehud Barak later described himself as having made the best possible offer that the Palestinians had ever been given. That offer apparently was to have Israel withdraw from eighty-eight percent or ninety-two percent (the offers were never in writing and conflicting versions were delivered verbally to PA President Arafat by Barak's representatives)—but it's important to remember this was ninety-two percent of the twenty-two percent of pre-48 Palestine. Since the Oslo Accord promises had been for the full twenty-two percent of the land to be returned (or at least that was what was informally conveyed to the PLO by Beilin), it was no wonder that the actual offer didn't seem to be so generous. In addition, Palestinians were not to be granted control over East Jerusalem contiguous with the Temple Mount and, as a result, the troops that prevented Muslims from praying at the Temple Mount would continue to be deployed. Finally, and most importantly, Barak insisted that the Palestinians agree to sign a statement that all issues between the two parties had been resolved. But meanwhile there was nothing in his offer that dealt with the fate of three million refugees. No Palestinian leader could have signed such an agreement.

What made the Camp David failure so damaging to the Palestinian cause was the prior and then subsequent failure of Arafat to convey a clear vision of what he actually would have settled for. This was a monumental misjudgment. Had Arafat put forward a real counter-offer and publicized it to the media, he might have offset the propaganda defeat the Palestinian people suffered. But without that, it was all too easy for those who sought to demean the Palestinians to say, "What we learned is that there is no real partner for peace because Arafat won't settle for anything."

In the aftermath of this fiasco, Ariel Sharon decided to take a walk on the Temple Mount, accompanied by hundreds of armed police, as a way of communicating symbolically that Israeli control over this sacred site (and perhaps the Occupation itself) would never end. When Palestinians threw rocks, Israeli troops opened fire with rubber bullets, and soon the rioting spread to East Jerusalem and to the Territories. Thus commenced Intifada II.

This second Intifada quickly escalated from the rocks of the first Intifada to armed conflict between two very unequally matched forces. On the one side was Israel, the fourth most powerful military in the world, bringing in tanks, helicopters, airplanes, and a well-trained and powerful army. On the other hand were the Palestinians with about 10,000 rifles and a few mortars. When Israel re-occupied Palestinian cities and met armed resistance, it was quickly suppressed. Palestinians then reverted to terror, with suicide bombers who proceeded to sneak across the border and murder innocent Israeli civilians.

During the Second Intifada, Ariel Sharon was able to effectively deploy his army to surround and isolate each Palestinian town or city and at times to impose 24-hour curfews that then went on for weeks. Hunger became rampant among the Palestinian population; malnutrition among children reached an estimated forty percent of the population.

The Israeli people also suffered and continue to suffer from the fear generated by the numerous suicide bombings in restaurants, cafes, buses, dance halls, and at religious gatherings and the fear generated by them. It is not my intention to make any judgments of "moral equivalency." From my standpoint, every unnecessary loss of life is a spiritual tragedy, and none of them can be made equivalent to any other. The suffering has been terrible, with escalating fear and unwillingness of people on both sides to allow themselves to imagine what the other is going through. By 2004 we are facing populations who are deeply distorted by not only their own suffering but their righteous anger toward those they believe are responsible for it.

The Coming of the Accord

When the Camp David negotiations failed, the world was told that the last best chance had been lost for making peace. Ehud Barak would face elections in February 2001. Having failed to achieve a breakthrough in negotiations, he was eager to portray the Palestinians as fundamentally intransigent and unreasonable.

Barak had been elected on the promise of making peace and, since to go to the elections utterly empty-handed was an acknowledgment of failure, he authorized further negotiations with the Palestinians, designating Yossi Beilin, the dovish Minister of Justice, to conduct them. Yasser Abed Rabbo, the Palestinian Authority's Minister of Information, was selected by the Palestinian Authority to represent Yasser Arafat. These two met at Taba and in the ensuing months unexpectedly made considerable progress toward a compromise acceptable to both sides. The negotiators reported in January that they were within a few weeks of reaching compromises on key issues. But they did not have those weeks. Barak swiftly cancelled the negotiations, and a few weeks later he was replaced by the victor in the Israeli elections, right-wing Likud leader Ariel Sharon. Sharon quickly announced that he had no further interest in the negotiations and that any concessions already offered by the State of Israel would no longer be binding since, he told the Israeli public, he had no intention of building upon the advances that had been made. Instead he would start with a clean slate should there ever be new negotiations. Of course, he knew this was impossible. He would stonewall as long as Yasser Arafat stayed as the leader of the Palestinian people.

Nevertheless, the key negotiators at Taba, Beilin and Abed Rabbo, continued to meet periodically during the next two years of the Intifada, and in the Fall of 2003 they announced that they had reached an agreement: the Geneva Accord. It was called "Geneva" in part because the group of people involved in these negotiations received financial backing and logistical support from the Swiss, and partly because some of the negotiations actually took place in Geneva.

What follows is the actual Accord. The document may be difficult to read. Being a version of an international treaty, it is filled with legalese. Read what you can, and skip to the following chapters that review the terms of the Accord, while discussing responses to and critiques of it.

2: The Geneva Accord

Preamble

The State of Israel (hereinafter "Israel") and the Palestine Liberation Organization (hereinafter "PLO"), the representative of the Palestinian people (hereinafter the "Parties"):

Reaffirming their determination to put an end to decades of confrontation and conflict, and to live in peaceful coexistence, mutual dignity and security based on a just, lasting, and comprehensive peace and achieving historic reconciliation;

Recognizing that peace requires the transition from the logic of war and confrontation to the logic of peace and cooperation, and that acts and words characteristic of the state of war are neither appropriate nor acceptable in the era of peace;

Affirming their deep belief that the logic of peace requires compromise, and that the only viable solution is a two-state solution based on UNSC Resolution 242 and 338;

Affirming that this agreement marks the recognition of the right of the Jewish people to statehood and the recognition of the right of the Palestinian people to statehood, without prejudice to the equal rights of the Parties' respective citizens;

Recognizing that after years of living in mutual fear and insecurity, both peoples need to enter an era of peace, security, and stability, entailing all necessary actions by the parties to guarantee the realization of this era;

Recognizing each other's right to peaceful and secure existence within secure and recognized boundaries free from threats or acts of force;

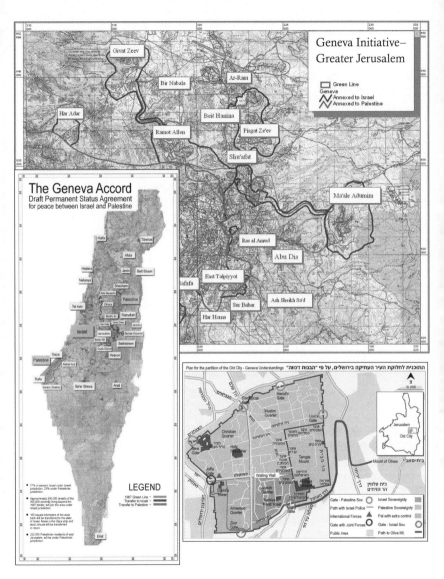

Geneva Initiative–
Greater Jerusalem

Green Line
Geneva
Annexed to Israel
Annexed to Palestine

Givat Zeev
Bir Nabala
Ar-Ram
Har Adar
Beit Hanina
Ramot Allon
Pisgat Ze'ev
Shu'afat
Ma'ale Adumim
Ras al Amud
Abu Dis
Safafa
East Talpiyyot
Sur Bahar
Ash Sheikh Sa'd
Har Homa

The Geneva Accord
Draft Permanent Status Agreement
for peace between Israel and Palestine

Haifa
Tiberias
Afula
Hadera
Jenin
Beit Shean
Netanya
Shechem
Alfei Menashe
Tel Aviv
Elkana
Palestine
Modi'in Ilit
Ramallah
Jerusalem
Har Adar
Givat Zeev
Jericho
Israel
Betar Illit
Ma'ale Adumim
Bethlehem
Gush Etzion
Hebron
Gaza
Palestine
Nahal Atz
Rafa
Kerem Shalom
Be'er Sheva
Arad

Eilat

- 77% of western Israeli under Israeli
  jurisdiction, 23% under Palestinian
  jurisdiction

- Approximately 300,000 Israelis of the
  400,000 currently living beyond the
  1967 border, will join the area under
  Israeli jurisdiction.

- 163 square kilometers of the west
  bank will be transferred to the state
  of Israel. Areas in the Gaza strip and
  west Jehuda will be transferred
  in return.

- 232,000 Palestinian residents of east
  Jerusalem, will be under Palestinian
  jurisdiction

LEGEND

1967 Green Line
Transfer to Israel
Transfer to Palestine

Plan for the partition of the Old City - Geneva Understandings   התוכנית לחלוקת העיר העתיקה בירושלים, על פי "הבנות דנוה"

Jerusalem
Old City

Damascus Gate
Herod's Gate
Lion's Gate
Muslim Quarter
Christian Quarter
New Gate
Holy Sepulcher
Temple Mount
Jaffa Gate
Mount of Olives
Walling Wall
Jewish Quarter
Armenian Quarter
Zion Gate
Path to Olive Mt.

Gate - Palestine Sov.   Israel Sovereignty
Path with Israel Police   Palestinian Sovereignty
International Forces   Pal with extra control
Gate with Joint Forces   Gate - Israel Sov.
Public Area   Path to Olive Mt.

21

Determined to establish relations based on cooperation and the commitment to live side by side as good neighbors aiming both separately and jointly to contribute to the well-being of their peoples;

Reaffirming their obligation to conduct themselves in conformity with the norms of international law and the Charter of the United Nations;

Confirming that this Agreement is concluded within the framework of the Middle East peace process initiated in Madrid in October 1991, the Declaration of Principles of September 13, 1993, the subsequent agreements including the Interim Agreement of September 1995, the Wye River Memorandum of October 1998 and the Sharm El-Sheikh Memorandum of September 4, 1999, and the permanent status negotiations including the Camp David Summit of July 2000, the Clinton Ideas of December 2000, and the Taba Negotiations of January 2001;

Reiterating their commitment to United Nations Security Council Resolutions 242, 338, and 1397 and confirming their understanding that this Agreement is based on, will lead to, and—by its fulfillment—will constitute the full implementation of these resolutions and to the settlement of the Israeli-Palestinian conflict in all its aspects;

Declaring that this Agreement constitutes the realization of the permanent status peace component envisaged in President Bush's speech of June 24, 2002 and in the Quartet Roadmap process;

Declaring that this Agreement marks the historic reconciliation between the Palestinians and Israelis, and paves the way to reconciliation between the Arab World and Israel and the establishment of normal, peaceful relations between the Arab states and Israel in accordance with the relevant clauses of the Beirut Arab League Resolution of March 28, 2002;

and

Resolved to pursue the goal of attaining a comprehensive regional peace, thus contributing to stability, security, development, and prosperity throughout the region;

Have agreed on the following:

Article 1—Purpose of the Permanent Status Agreement
1. The Permanent Status Agreement (hereinafter "this Agreement") ends the era of conflict and ushers in a new era based on peace, cooperation, and good neighborly relations between the Parties.
2. The implementation of this Agreement will settle all the claims of the Parties arising from events occurring prior to its signature. No further claims related to events prior to this Agreement may be raised by either Party.

Article 2—Relations between the Parties
1. The state of Israel shall recognize the state of Palestine (hereinafter "Palestine") upon its establishment. The state of Palestine shall immediately recognize the state of Israel.
2. The state of Palestine shall be the successor to the PLO with all its rights and obligations.
3. Israel and Palestine shall immediately establish full diplomatic and consular relations with each other and will exchange resident Ambassadors, within one month of their mutual recognition.
4. The Parties recognize Palestine and Israel as the homelands of their respective peoples. The Parties are committed not to interfere in each other's internal affairs.
5. This Agreement supercedes all prior agreements between the Parties.
6. Without prejudice to the commitments undertaken by them in this Agreement, relations between Israel and Palestine shall be based upon the provisions of the Charter of the United Nations.

7. With a view to the advancement of the relations between the two States and peoples, Palestine and Israel shall cooperate in areas of common interest. These shall include, but are not limited to, dialogue between their legislatures and state institutions, cooperation between their appropriate local authorities, promotion of non-governmental civil society cooperation, and joint programs and exchange in the areas of culture, media, youth, science, education, environment, health, agriculture, tourism, and crime prevention. The Israeli-Palestinian Cooperation Committee will oversee this cooperation in accordance with Article 8.

8. The Parties shall cooperate in areas of joint economic interest, to best realize the human potential of their respective peoples. In this regard, they will work bilaterally, regionally, and with the international community to maximize the benefit of peace to the broadest cross-section of their respective populations. Relevant standing bodies shall be established by the Parties to this effect.

9. The Parties shall establish robust modalities for security cooperation, and engage in a comprehensive and uninterrupted effort to end terrorism and violence directed against each others persons, property, institutions or territory. This effort shall continue at all times, and shall be insulated from any possible crises and other aspects of the Parties' relations.

10. Israel and Palestine shall work together and separately with other parties in the region to enhance and promote regional cooperation and coordination in spheres of common interest.

11. The Parties shall establish a ministerial-level Palestinian-Israeli High Steering Committee to guide, monitor, and facilitate the process of implementation of this Agreement, both bilaterally and in accordance with the mechanisms in Article 3 hereunder.

Article 3: Implementation and Verification Group

1. Establishment and Composition

    (a) An Implementation and Verification Group (IVG) shall hereby be established to facilitate, assist in, guarantee, monitor, and resolve disputes relating to the implementation of this Agreement.

    (b) The IVG shall include the U.S., the Russian Federation, the EU, the UN, and other parties, both regional and international, to be agreed on by the Parties.

    (c) The IVG shall work in coordination with the Palestinian-Israeli High Steering Committee established in Article 2/11 above and subsequent to that with the Israeli-Palestinian Cooperation Committee (IPCC) established in Article 8 hereunder.

    (d) The structure, procedures, and modalities of the IVG are set forth below and detailed in Annex X.

2. Structure

    (a) A senior political-level contact group (Contact Group), composed of all the IVG members, shall be the highest authority in the IVG.

    (b) The Contact Group shall appoint, in consultation with the Parties, a Special Representative who will be the principal executive of the IVG on the ground. The Special Representative shall manage the work of the IVG and maintain constant contact with the Parties, the Palestinian-Israeli High Steering Committee, and the Contact Group.

    (c) The IVG permanent headquarters and secretariat shall be based in an agreed upon location in Jerusalem.

    (d) The IVG shall establish its bodies referred to in this Agreement and additional bodies as it deems necessary. These bodies shall be an integral part of and under the authority of the IVG.

    (e) The Multinational Force (MF) established under Article 5 shall be an integral part of the IVG. The Special Representative shall, subject to the approval of the Parties, appoint the Commander of the MF who shall be responsible for the daily command of the MF. Details relating to the Special Representative and MF Force Commander are set forth in Annex X.

(f) The IVG shall establish a dispute settlement mechanism, in accordance with Article 16.

3. Coordination with the Parties. A Trilateral Committee composed of the Special Representative and the Palestinian-Israeli High Steering Committee shall be established and shall meet on at least a monthly basis to review the implementation of this Agreement. The Trilateral Committee will convene within 48 hours upon the request of any of the three parties represented.

4. Functions. In addition to the functions specified elsewhere in this Agreement, the IVG shall: (a) Take appropriate measures based on the reports it receives from the MF, (b) Assist the Parties in implementing the Agreement and preempt and promptly mediate disputes on the ground.

5. Termination. In accordance with the progress in the implementation of this Agreement, and with the fulfillment of the specific mandated functions, the IVG shall terminate its activities in the said spheres. The IVG shall continue to exist unless otherwise agreed by the Parties.

Article 4—Territory

1. The International Borders between the States of Palestine and Israel

   (a) In accordance with UNSC Resolution 242 and 338, the border between the states of Palestine and Israel shall be based on the June 4th 1967 lines with reciprocal modifications on a 1:1 basis as set forth in attached Map 1.

   (b) The Parties recognize the border, as set out in attached Map 1, as the permanent, secure, and recognized international boundary between them.

2. Sovereignty and Inviolability

　(a) The Parties recognize and respect each other's sovereignty, territorial integrity, and political independence, as well as the inviolability of each others territory, including territorial waters, and airspace. They shall respect this inviolability in accordance with this Agreement, the UN Charter, and other rules of international law.

　(b) The Parties recognize each other's rights in their exclusive economic zones in accordance with international law.

3. Israeli Withdrawal

　(a) Israel shall withdraw in accordance with Article 5.

　(b) Palestine shall assume responsibility for the areas from which Israel withdraws.

　(c) The transfer of authority from Israel to Palestine shall be in accordance with Annex X.

　(d) The IVG shall monitor, verify, and facilitate the implementation of this Article.

4. Demarcation

　(a) A Joint Technical Border Commission (Commission) composed of the two Parties shall be established to conduct the technical demarcation of the border in accordance with this Article. The procedures governing the work of this Commission are set forth in Annex X.

　(b) Any disagreement in the Commission shall be referred to the IVG in accordance with Annex X.

　(c) The physical demarcation of the international borders shall be completed by the Commission not later than nine months from the date of the entry into force of this Agreement.

5. Settlements

   (a) The state of Israel shall be responsible for resettling the Israelis residing in Palestinian sovereign territory outside this territory.

   (b) The resettlement shall be completed according to the schedule stipulated in Article 5.

   (c) Existing arrangements in the West Bank and Gaza Strip regarding Israeli settlers and settlements, including security, shall remain in force in each of the settlements until the date prescribed in the timetable for the completion of the evacuation of the relevant settlement.

   (d) Modalities for the assumption of authority over settlements by Palestine are set forth in Annex X. The IVG shall resolve any disputes that may arise during its implementation.

   (e) Israel shall keep intact the immovable property, infrastructure and facilities in Israeli settlements to be transferred to Palestinian sovereignty. An agreed inventory shall be drawn up by the Parties with the IVG in advance of the completion of the evacuation and in accordance with Annex X.

   (f) The state of Palestine shall have exclusive title to all land and any buildings, facilities, infrastructure or other property remaining in any of the settlements on the date prescribed in the timetable for the completion of the evacuation of this settlement.

6. Corridor

   (a) The states of Palestine and Israel shall establish a corridor linking the West Bank and Gaza Strip. This corridor shall:

      i. Be under Israeli sovereignty.

      ii. Be permanently open.

      iii. Be under Palestinian administration in accordance with Annex X of this Agreement. Palestinian law shall apply to persons using and procedures appertaining to the corridor.

    iv. Not disrupt Israeli transportation and other infrastructural networks, or endanger the environment, public safety or public health. Where necessary, engineering solutions will be sought to avoid such disruptions.

    v. Allow for the establishment of the necessary infrastructural facilities linking the West Bank and the Gaza Strip. Infrastructural facilities shall be understood to include, inter alia, pipelines, electrical and communications cables, and associated equipment as detailed in Annex X.

    vi. Not be used in contravention of this Agreement.

(b) Defensive barriers shall be established along the corridor and Palestinians shall not enter Israel from this corridor, nor shall Israelis enter Palestine from the corridor.

(c) The Parties shall seek the assistance of the international community in securing the financing for the corridor.

(d) The IVG shall guarantee the implementation of this Article in accordance with Annex X.

(e) Any disputes arising between the Parties from the operation of the corridor shall be resolved in accordance with Article 16.

(f) The arrangements set forth in this clause may only be terminated or revised by agreement of both Parties.

Article 5—Security

1. General Security Provisions

(a) The Parties acknowledge that mutual understanding and cooperation in security-related matters will form a significant part of their bilateral relations and will further enhance regional security. Palestine and Israel shall base their security relations on cooperation, mutual trust, good neighborly relations, and the protection of their joint interests.

(b) Palestine and Israel each shall:

    i. Recognize and respect the other's right to live in peace within secure and recognized boundaries free from the threat or acts of war, terrorism and violence;

    ii. refrain from the threat or use of force against the territorial integrity or political independence of the other and shall settle all disputes between them by peaceful means;

    iii. refrain from joining, assisting, promoting or co-operating with any coalition, organization or alliance of a military or security character, the objectives or activities of which include launching aggression or other acts of hostility against the other;

    iv. refrain from organizing, encouraging, or allowing the formation of irregular forces or armed bands, including mercenaries and militias within their respective territory and prevent their establishment. In this respect, any existing irregular forces or armed bands shall be disbanded and prevented from reforming at any future date;

    v. refrain from organizing, assisting, allowing, or participating in acts of violence in or against the other or acquiescing in activities directed toward the commission of such acts.

(c) To further security cooperation, the Parties shall establish a high level Joint Security Committee that shall meet on at least a monthly basis. The Joint Security Committee shall have a permanent joint office, and may establish such sub-committees as it deems necessary, including sub-committees to immediately resolve localized tensions.

2. Regional Security

    i. Israel and Palestine shall work together with their neighbors and the international community to build a secure and stable Middle East, free from weapons of mass destruction, both conventional and non-conventional, in the context of a comprehensive, lasting, and stable peace, characterized by rec-

onciliation, goodwill, and the renunciation of the use of force.
ii. To this end, the Parties shall work together to establish a regional security regime.

3. Defense Characteristics of the Palestinian State

   (a) No armed forces, other than as specified in this Agreement, will be deployed or stationed in Palestine.

   (b) Palestine shall be a non-militarized state, with a strong security force. Accordingly, the limitations on the weapons that may be purchased, owned, or used by the Palestinian Security Force (PSF) or manufactured in Palestine shall be specified in Annex X. Any proposed changes to Annex X shall be considered by a trilateral committee composed of the two Parties and the MF. If no agreement is reached in the trilateral committee, the IVG may make its own recommendations. i. No individuals or organizations in Palestine other than the PSF and the organs of the IVG, including the MF, may purchase, possess, carry or use weapons except as provided by law.

   (c) The PSF shall: i. Maintain border control; ii. Maintain law-and-order and perform police functions; iii. Perform intelligence and security functions; iv. Prevent terrorism; v. Conduct rescue and emergency missions; and vi. Supplement essential community services when necessary.

   (d) The MF shall monitor and verify compliance with this clause.

4. Terrorism

   (a) The Parties reject and condemn terrorism and violence in all its forms and shall pursue public policies accordingly. In addition, the parties shall refrain from actions and policies that are liable to nurture extremism and create conditions conducive to terrorism on either side.

   (b) The Parties shall take joint and, in their respective territories, unilateral comprehensive and continuous efforts against all aspects of violence and terrorism. These efforts shall include the prevention and preemption of such acts, and the prosecution of their perpetrators.

(c) To that end, the Parties shall maintain ongoing consultation, cooperation, and exchange of information between their respective security forces.

(d) A Trilateral Security Committee composed of the two Parties and the United States shall be formed to ensure the implementation of this Article. The Trilateral Security Committee shall develop comprehensive policies and guidelines to fight terrorism and violence.

5. Incitement

(a) Without prejudice to freedom of expression and other internationally recognized human rights, Israel and Palestine shall promulgate laws to prevent incitement to irredentism, racism, terrorism, and violence and vigorously enforce them.

(b) The IVG shall assist the Parties in establishing guidelines for the implementation of this clause, and shall monitor the Parties' adherence thereto.

6. Multinational Force

(a) A Multinational Force (MF) shall be established to provide security guarantees to the Parties, act as a deterrent, and oversee the implementation of the relevant provisions of this Agreement.

(b) The composition, structure, and size of the MF are set forth in Annex X.

(c) To perform the functions specified in this Agreement, the MF shall be deployed in the state of Palestine. The MF shall enter into the appropriate Status of Forces Agreement (SOFA) with the state of Palestine.

(d) In accordance with this Agreement, and as detailed in Annex X, the MF shall:

    i. In light of the non-militarized nature of the Palestinian state,
       protect the territorial integrity of the state of Palestine.
   ii. Serve as a deterrent against external attacks that could
       threaten either of the Parties.
  iii. Deploy observers to areas adjacent to the lines of the Israeli
       withdrawal during the phases of this withdrawal, in accor-
       dance with Annex X.
   iv. Deploy observers to monitor the territorial and maritime bor-
       ders of the state of Palestine, as specified in clause 5/13.
    v. Perform the functions on the Palestinian international bor-
       der crossings specified in clause 5/12.
   vi. Perform the functions relating to the early warning stations
       as specified in clause 5/8.
  vii. Perform the functions specified in clause 5/3.
 viii. Perform the functions specified in clause 5/7.
   ix. Perform the functions specified in Article 10.
    x. Help in the enforcement of anti-terrorism measures.
   xi. Help in the training of the PSF.
  (e) In relation to the above, the MF shall report to and update the
      IVG in accordance with Annex X.
  (f) The MF shall only be withdrawn or have its mandate changed by
      agreement of the Parties.
7. Evacuation
  (a) Israel shall withdraw all its military and security personnel and
      equipment, including landmines, and all persons employed to
      support them, and all military installations from the territory
      of the state of Palestine, except as otherwise agreed in Annex
      X, in stages.
  (b) The staged withdrawals shall commence immediately upon
      entry into force of this Agreement and shall be made in accor-
      dance with the timetable and modalities set forth in Annex X.

(c) The stages shall be designed subject to the following principles:

    i. The need to create immediate clear contiguity and facilitate the early implementation of Palestinian development plans.

    ii. Israel's capacity to relocate, house, and absorb settlers. While costs and inconveniences are inherent in such a process, these shall not be unduly disruptive.

    iii. The need to construct and operationalize the border between the two states.

    iv. The introduction and effective functioning of the MF, in particular on the eastern border of the state of Palestine.

(d) Accordingly, the withdrawal shall be implemented in the following stages:

    i. The first stage shall include the areas of the state of Palestine, as defined in Map X, and shall be completed within 9 months.

    ii. The second and third stages shall include the remainder of the territory of the state of Palestine and shall be completed within 21 months of the end of the first stage.

(e) Israel shall complete its withdrawal from the territory of the state of Palestine within 30 months of the entry into force of this Agreement, and in accordance with this Agreement.

(f) Israel will maintain a small military presence in the Jordan Valley under the authority of the MF and subject to the MF SOFA as detailed in Annex X for an additional 36 months. The stipulated period may be reviewed by the Parties in the event of relevant regional developments, and may be altered by the Parties' consent.

(g) In accordance with Annex X, the MF shall monitor and verify compliance with this clause.

8. Early Warning Stations

(a) Israel may maintain two EWS in the northern, and central West

Bank at the locations set forth in Annex X.

(b) The EWS shall be staffed by the minimal required number of Israeli personnel and shall occupy the minimal amount of land necessary for their operation as set forth in Annex X.

(c) Access to the EWS will be guaranteed and escorted by the MF.

(d) Internal security of the EWS shall be the responsibility of Israel. The perimeter security of the EWS shall be the responsibility of the MF.

(e) The MF and the PSF shall maintain a liaison presence in the EWS. The MF shall monitor and verify that the EWS is being used for purposes recognized by this Agreement as detailed in Annex X.

(f) The arrangements set forth in this Article shall be subject to review in ten years, with any changes to be mutually agreed. Thereafter, there will be five-yearly reviews whereby the arrangements set forth in this Article may be extended by mutual consent.

(g) If at any point during the period specified above a regional security regime is established, then the IVG may request that the Parties review whether to continue or revise operational uses for the EWS in light of these developments. Any such change will require the mutual consent of the Parties.

9. Airspace

   (a) Civil Aviation

      i. The Parties recognize as applicable to each other the rights, privileges and obligations provided for by the multilateral aviation agreements to which they are both party, particularly by the 1944 Convention on International Civil Aviation (The Chicago Convention) and the 1944 International Air Services Transit Agreement.

      ii. In addition, the Parties shall, upon entry into force of this

Agreement, establish a trilateral committee composed of the two Parties and the IVG to design the most efficient management system for civil aviation, including those relevant aspects of the air traffic control system. In the absence of consensus the IVG may make its own recommendations.

(b) Training

    i. The Israeli Air Force shall be entitled to use the Palestinian sovereign airspace for training purposes in accordance with Annex X, which shall be based on rules pertaining to IAF use of Israeli airspace.

    ii. The IVG shall monitor and verify compliance with this clause. Either Party may submit a complaint to the IVG whose decision shall be conclusive.

    iii. The arrangements set forth in this clause shall be subject to review every ten years, and may be altered or terminated by the agreement of both Parties.

10. Electromagnetic Sphere

(a) Neither Party's use of the electromagnetic sphere may interfere with the other Party's use.

(b) Annex X shall detail arrangements relating to the use of the electromagnetic sphere.

(c) The IVG shall monitor and verify the implementation of this clause and Annex X.

(d) Any Party may submit a complaint to the IVG whose decision shall be conclusive.

11. Law Enforcement. The Israeli and Palestinian law enforcement agencies shall cooperate in combating illicit drug trafficking, illegal trafficking in archaeological artifacts and objects of arts, cross-border crime, including theft and fraud, organized crime, trafficking in women and minors, counterfeiting, pirate TV and radio stations, and other illegal activity.

12. International Border Crossings
    (a) The following arrangements shall apply to borders crossing
        between the state of Palestine and Jordan, the state of Palestine
        and Egypt, as well as airport and seaport entry points to the
        state of Palestine.
    (b) All border crossings shall be monitored by joint teams com-
        posed of members of the PSF and the MF. These teams shall
        prevent the entry into Palestine of any weapons, materials, or
        equipment that are in contravention of the provisions of this
        Agreement.
    (c) The MF representatives and the PSF will have, jointly and sep-
        arately, the authority to block the entry into Palestine of any
        such items. If at any time a disagreement regarding the entrance
        of goods or materials arises between the PSF and the MF rep-
        resentatives, the PSF may bring the matter to the IVG, whose
        binding conclusions shall be rendered within 24 hours.
    (d) This arrangement shall be reviewed by the IVG after 5 years to
        determine its continuation, modification or termination. There-
        after, the Palestinian party may request such a review on an
        annual basis.
    (e) In passenger terminals, for thirty months, Israel may maintain
        an unseen presence in a designated on-site facility, to be staffed
        by members of the MF and Israelis, utilizing appropriate tech-
        nology. The Israeli side may request that the MF-PSF conduct
        further inspections and take appropriate action.
    (f) For the following two years, these arrangements will continue
        in a specially designated facility in Israel, utilizing appropriate
        technology. This shall not cause delays beyond the procedures
        outlined in this clause.
    (g) In cargo terminals, for thirty months, Israel may maintain an
        unseen presence in a designated on-site facility, to be staffed by

members of the MF and Israelis, utilizing appropriate technology. The Israeli side may request that the MF-PSF conduct further inspections and take appropriate action. If the Israeli side is not satisfied by the MF-PSF action, it may demand that the cargo be detained pending a decision by an MF inspector. The MF inspector's decision shall be binding and final, and shall be rendered within 12 hours of the Israeli complaint.

(h) For the following three years, these arrangements will continue from a specially designated facility in Israel, utilizing appropriate technology. This shall not cause delays beyond the timelines outlined in this clause.

(i) A high level trilateral committee composed of representatives of Palestine, Israel, and the IVG shall meet regularly to monitor the application of these procedures and correct any irregularities, and may be convened on request.

(j) The details of the above are set forth in Annex X.

13. Border Control

(a) The PSF shall maintain border control as detailed in Annex X.

(b) The MF shall monitor and verify the maintenance of border control by the PSF.

Article 6—Jerusalem

1. Religious and Cultural Significance:

(a) The Parties recognize the universal historic, religious, spiritual, and cultural significance of Jerusalem and its holiness enshrined in Judaism, Christianity, and Islam. In recognition of this status, the Parties reaffirm their commitment to safeguard the character, holiness, and freedom of worship in the city and to respect the existing division of administrative functions and traditional practices between different denominations.

(b) The Parties shall establish an inter-faith body consisting of representatives of the three monotheistic faiths, to act as a consultative body to the Parties on matters related to the city's religious significance and to promote inter-religious understanding and dialogue. The composition, procedures, and modalities for this body are set forth in Annex X.

2. Capital of Two States. The Parties shall have their mutually recognized capitals in the areas of Jerusalem under their respective sovereignty.

3. Sovereignty in Jerusalem shall be in accordance with attached Map 2. This shall not prejudice nor be prejudiced by the arrangements set forth below.

4. Border Regime. The border regime shall be designed according to the provisions of Article 11, and taking into account the specific needs of Jerusalem (e.g., movement of tourists and intensity of border crossing use including provisions for Jerusalemites) and the provisions of this Article.

5. al-Haram al-Sharif/Temple Mount (Compound)

(a) International Group

i. An International Group, composed of the IVG and other parties to be agreed upon by the Parties, including members of the Organization of the Islamic Conference (OIC), shall hereby be established to monitor, verify, and assist in the implementation of this clause.

ii. For this purpose, the International Group shall establish a Multinational Presence on the Compound, the composition, structure, mandate and functions of which are set forth in Annex X.

iii. The Multinational Presence shall have specialized detachments dealing with security and conservation. The Multinational Presence shall make periodic conservation and security reports to the International Group. These reports shall be made public.

iv. The Multinational Presence shall strive to immediately resolve any problems arising and may refer any unresolved disputes to the International Group that will function in accordance with Article 16.

v. The Parties may at any time request clarifications or submit complaints to the International Group which shall be promptly investigated and acted upon.

vi. The International Group shall draw up rules and regulations to maintain security on and conservation of the Compound. These shall include lists of the weapons and equipment permitted on the site.

(b) Regulations Regarding the Compound

i. In view of the sanctity of the Compound, and in light of the unique religious and cultural significance of the site to the Jewish people, there shall be no digging, excavation, or construction on the Compound, unless approved by the two Parties. Procedures for regular maintenance and emergency repairs on the Compound shall be established by the IG after consultation with the Parties.

ii. The state of Palestine shall be responsible for maintaining the security of the Compound and for ensuring that it will not be used for any hostile acts against Israelis or Israeli areas. The only arms permitted on the Compound shall be those carried by the Palestinian security personnel and the security detachment of the Multinational Presence.

iii. In light of the universal significance of the Compound, and subject to security considerations and to the need not to disrupt religious worship or decorum on the site as determined by the Waqf, visitors shall be allowed access to the site. This shall be without any discrimination and generally be in accor-

dance with past practice.
  (c) Transfer of Authority
      i. At the end of the withdrawal period stipulated in Article
         5/7, the state of Palestine shall assert sovereignty over the
         Compound.
      ii. The International Group and its subsidiary organs shall con-
          tinue to exist and fulfill all the functions stipulated in this
          Article unless otherwise agreed by the two Parties.
6. The Wailing Wall. The Wailing Wall shall be under Israeli sovereignty.
7. The Old City
   (a) Significance of the Old City
       i. The Parties view the Old City as one whole enjoying a unique
          character. The Parties agree that the preservation of this
          unique character together with safeguarding and promoting
          the welfare of the inhabitants should guide the administra-
          tion of the Old City.
       ii. The Parties shall act in accordance with the UNESCO World
           Cultural Heritage List regulations, in which the Old City is
           a registered site.
   (b) IVG Role in the Old City
       i. Cultural Heritage 1. The IVG shall monitor and verify the
          preservation of cultural heritage in the Old City in accor-
          dance with the UNESCO World Cultural Heritage List rules.
          For this purpose, the IVG shall have free and unimpeded
          access to sites, documents, and information related to the
          performance of this function. 2. The IVG shall work in close
          coordination with the Old City Committee of the Jerusalem
          Coordination and Development Committee (JCDC), includ-
          ing in devising a restoration and preservation plan for the
          Old City.

41

ii. Policing 1. The IVG shall establish an Old City Policing Unit (PU) to liaise with, coordinate between, and assist the Palestinian and Israeli police forces in the Old City, to defuse localized tensions and help resolve disputes, and to perform policing duties in locations specified in and according to operational procedures detailed in Annex X. 2. The PU shall periodically report to the IVG.

iii. Either Party may submit complaints in relation to this clause to the IVG, which shall promptly act upon them in accordance with Article 16.

(c) Free Movement within the Old City Movement within the Old City shall be free and unimpeded subject to the provisions of this article and rules and regulations pertaining to the various holy sites.

(d) Entry into and Exit from the Old City

i. Entry and exit points into and from the Old City will be staffed by the authorities of the state under whose sovereignty the point falls, with the presence of PU members, unless otherwise specified.

ii. With a view to facilitating movement into the Old City, each Party shall take such measures at the entry points in its territory as to ensure the preservation of security in the Old City. The PU shall monitor the operation of the entry points.

iii. Citizens of either Party may not exit the Old City into the territory of the other Party unless they are in possession of the relevant documentation that entitles them to. Tourists may only exit the Old City into the territory of the Party which they possess valid authorization to enter.

(e) Suspension, Termination, and Expansion

i. Either Party may suspend the arrangements set forth in Article 6.7.iii in cases of emergency for one week. The extension of such suspension for longer than a week shall be pursuant to consultation with the other Party and the IVG at the Trilateral Committee established in Article 3/3.

ii. This clause shall not apply to the arrangements set forth in Article 6/7/vi.

iii. Three years after the transfer of authority over the Old City, the Parties shall review these arrangements. These arrangements may only be terminated by agreement of the Parties.

iv. The Parties shall examine the possibility of expanding these arrangements beyond the Old City and may agree to such an expansion.

(f) Special Arrangements

i. Along the way outlined in Map X (from the Jaffa Gate to the Zion Gate) there will be permanent and guaranteed arrangements for Israelis regarding access, freedom of movement, and security, as set forth in Annex X. 1. The IVG shall be responsible for the implementation of these arrangements.

ii. Without prejudice to Palestinian sovereignty, Israeli administration of the Citadel will be as outlined in Annex X.

(g) Color-Coding of the Old City. A visible color-coding scheme shall be used in the Old City to denote the sovereign areas of the respective Parties.

(h) Policing

i. An agreed number of Israeli police shall constitute the Israeli Old City police detachment and shall exercise responsibility for maintaining order and day-to-day policing functions in the area under Israeli sovereignty.

ii. An agreed number of Palestinian police shall constitute the Palestinian Old City police detachment and shall exercise responsibility for maintaining order and day-to-day policing functions in the area under Palestinian sovereignty.

      iii. All members of the respective Israeli and Palestinian Old City police detachments shall undergo special training, including joint training exercises, to be administered by the PU.

      iv. A special Joint Situation Room, under the direction of the PU and incorporating members of the Israeli and Palestinian Old City police detachments, shall facilitate liaison on all relevant matters of policing and security in the Old City.

(i) Arms. No person shall be allowed to carry or possess arms in the Old City, with the exception of the Police Forces provided for in this agreement. In addition, each Party may grant special written permission to carry or possess arms in areas under its sovereignty.

(j) Intelligence and Security

      i. The Parties shall establish intensive intelligence cooperation regarding the Old City, including the immediate sharing of threat information.

      ii. A trilateral committee composed of the two Parties and representatives of the United States shall be established to facilitate this cooperation.

8. Mount of Olives Cemetery

(a) The area outlined in Map X (the Jewish Cemetery on the Mount of Olives) shall be under Israeli administration; Israeli law shall apply to persons using and procedures appertaining to this area in accordance with Annex X.

      i. There shall be a designated road to provide free, unlimited, and unimpeded access to the Cemetery.

      ii. The IVG shall monitor the implementation of this clause.

      iii. This arrangement may only be terminated by the agreement of both Parties.

9. Special Cemetery Arrangements shall be established in the two cemeteries designated in Map X (Mount Zion Cemetery and the

German Colony Cemetery), to facilitate and ensure the continuation of the current burial and visitation practices, including the facilitation of access.

10. The Western Wall Tunnel
    (a) The Western Wall Tunnel designated in Map X shall be under Israeli administration, including: i. Unrestricted Israeli access and right to worship and conduct religious practices. ii. Responsibility for the preservation and maintenance of the site in accordance with this Agreement and without damaging structures above, under IVG supervision. iii. Israeli policing. iv. IVG monitoring v. The Northern Exit of the Tunnel shall only be used for exit and may only be closed in case of emergency as stipulated in Article 6/7.
    (b) This arrangement may only be terminated by the agreement of both Parties.

11. Municipal Coordination
    (a) The two Jerusalem municipalities shall form a Jerusalem Coordination and Development Committee ("JCDC") to oversee the cooperation and coordination between the Palestinian Jerusalem municipality and the Israeli Jerusalem municipality. The JCDC and its sub-committees shall be composed of an equal number of representatives from Palestine and Israel. Each side will appoint members of the JCDC and its subcommittees in accordance with its own modalities.
    (b) The JCDC shall ensure that the coordination of infrastructure and services best serves the residents of Jerusalem, and shall promote the economic development of the city to the benefit of all. The JCDC will act to encourage cross-community dialogue and reconciliation.
    (c) The JCDC shall have the following subcommittees:
        i. A Planning and Zoning Committee: to ensure agreed plan-

ning and zoning regulations in areas designated in Annex X.

ii. A Hydro Infrastructure Committee: to handle matters relating to drinking water delivery, drainage, and wastewater collection and treatment.

iii. A Transport Committee: to coordinate relevant connectedness and compatibility of the two road systems and other issues pertaining to transport.

iv. An Environmental Committee: to deal with environmental issues affecting the quality of life in the city, including solid waste management.

v. An Economic and Development Committee: to formulate plans for economic development in areas of joint interest, including in the areas of transportation, seam line commercial cooperation, and tourism.

vi. A Police and Emergency Services Committee: to coordinate measures for the maintenance of public order and crime prevention and the provision of emergency services;

vii. An Old City Committee: to plan and closely coordinate the joint provision of the relevant municipal services, and other functions stipulated in Article 6/7.

viii. Other Committees as agreed in the JCDC.

12. Israeli Residency of Palestinian Jerusalemites. Palestinian Jerusalemites who currently are permanent residents of Israel shall lose this status upon the transfer of authority to Palestine of those areas in which they reside.

13. Transfer of authority. The Parties will apply in certain socio-economic spheres interim measures to ensure the agreed, expeditious, and orderly transfer of powers and obligations from Israel to Palestine. This shall be done in a manner that preserves the accumulated socio-economic rights of the residents of East Jerusalem.

Article 7—Refugees
1. Significance of the Refugee Problem
    (a) The Parties recognize that, in the context of two independent states, Palestine and Israel, living side by side in peace, an agreed resolution of the refugee problem is necessary for achieving a just, comprehensive and lasting peace between them.
    (b) Such a resolution will also be central to stability building and development in the region.
2. UNGAR 194, UNSC Resolution 242, and the Arab Peace Initiative
    (a) The Parties recognize that UNGAR 194, UNSC Resolution 242, and the Arab Peace Initiative (Article 2.ii.) concerning the rights of the Palestinian refugees represent the basis for resolving the refugee issue, and agree that these rights are fulfilled according to Article 7 of this Agreement.
3. Compensation
    (a) Refugees shall be entitled to compensation for their refugeehood and for loss of property. This shall not prejudice or be prejudiced by the refugee's permanent place of residence.
    (b) The Parties recognize the right of states that have hosted Palestinian refugees to remuneration.
4. Choice of Permanent Place of Residence (PPR). The solution to the PPR aspect of the refugee problem shall entail an act of informed choice on the part of the refugee to be exercised in accordance with the options and modalities set forth in this agreement. PPR options from which the refugees may choose shall be as follows;
    (a) The state of Palestine, in accordance with clause a below.
    (b) Areas in Israel being transferred to Palestine in the land swap, following assumption of Palestinian sovereignty, in accordance with clause a below.
    (c) Third Countries, in accordance with clause b below.

(d) The state of Israel, in accordance with clause c below.
(e) Present Host countries, in accordance with clause d below.
    i. PPR options i and ii shall be the right of all Palestinian refugees and shall be in accordance with the laws of the State of Palestine.
    ii. Option iii shall be at the sovereign discretion of third countries and shall be in accordance with numbers that each third country will submit to the International Commission. These numbers shall represent the total number of Palestinian refugees that each third country shall accept.
    iii. Option iv shall be at the sovereign discretion of Israel and will be in accordance with a number that Israel will submit to the International Commission. This number shall represent the total number of Palestinian refugees that Israel shall accept. As a basis, Israel will consider the average of the total numbers submitted by the different third countries to the International Commission.
    iv. Option v shall be in accordance with the sovereign discretion of present host countries. Where exercised this shall be in the context of prompt and extensive development and rehabilitation programs for the refugee communities.

Priority in all the above shall be accorded to the Palestinian refugee population in Lebanon.

5. Free and Informed Choice. The process by which Palestinian refugees shall express their PPR choice shall be on the basis of a free and informed decision. The Parties themselves are committed and will encourage third parties to facilitate the refugees' free choice in expressing their preferences, and to countering any attempts at interference or organized pressure on the process of choice. This will not prejudice the recognition of Palestine as the realization of Palestinian self-determination and statehood.

6. End of Refugee Status. Palestinian refugee status shall be terminated upon the realization of an individual refugee's permanent place of residence (PPR) as determined by the International Commission.

7. End of Claims. This agreement provides for the permanent and complete resolution of the Palestinian refugee problem. No claims may be raised except for those related to the implementation of this agreement.

8. International Role. The Parties call upon the international community to participate fully in the comprehensive resolution of the refugee problem in accordance with this Agreement, including, inter alia, the establishment of an International Commission and an International Fund.

9. Property Compensation
   (a) Refugees shall be compensated for the loss of property resulting from their displacement.
   (b) The aggregate sum of property compensation shall be calculated as follows:
      i. The Parties shall request the International Commission to appoint a Panel of Experts to estimate the value of Palestinians' property at the time of displacement.
      ii. The Panel of Experts shall base its assessment on the UNCCP records, the records of the Custodian for Absentee Property, and any other records it deems relevant. The Parties shall make these records available to the Panel.
      iii. The Parties shall appoint experts to advise and assist the Panel in its work.
      iv. Within 6 months, the Panel shall submit its estimates to the Parties.
      v. The Parties shall agree on an economic multiplier, to be applied to the estimates, to reach a fair aggregate value of

the property.

(c) The aggregate value agreed to by the Parties shall constitute the Israeli "lump sum" contribution to the International Fund. No other financial claims arising from the Palestinian refugee problem may be raised against Israel.

(d) Israel's contribution shall be made in installments in accordance with Schedule X.

(e) The value of the Israeli fixed assets that shall remain intact in former settlements and transferred to the state of Palestine will be deducted from Israel's contribution to the International Fund. An estimation of this value shall be made by the International Fund, taking into account assessment of damage caused by the settlements.

10. Compensation for Refugeehood

(a) A "Refugeehood Fund" shall be established in recognition of each individual's refugeehood. The Fund, to which Israel shall be a contributing party, shall be overseen by the International Commission. The structure and financing of the Fund is set forth in Annex X.

(b) Funds will be disbursed to refugee communities in the former areas of UNRWA operation, and will be at their disposal for communal development and commemoration of the refugee experience. Appropriate mechanisms will be devised by the International Commission whereby the beneficiary refugee communities are empowered to determine and administer the use of this Fund.

11. The International Commission (Commission)

(a) Mandate and Composition

i. An International Commission shall be established and shall have full and exclusive responsibility for implementing all aspects of this Agreement pertaining to refugees.

ii. In addition to themselves, the Parties call upon the United Nations, the United States, UNRWA, the Arab host countries, the EU, Switzerland, Canada, Norway, Japan, the World Bank, the Russian Federation, and others to be the members of the Commission.

iii. The Commission shall: 1. Oversee and manage the process whereby the status and PPR of Palestinian refugees is determined and realized. 2. Oversee and manage, in close cooperation with the host states, the rehabilitation and development programs. 3. Raise and disburse funds as appropriate.

iv. The Parties shall make available to the Commission all relevant documentary records and archival materials in their possession that it deems necessary for the functioning of the Commission and its organs. The Commission may request such materials from all other relevant parties and bodies, including, inter alia, UNCCP, and UNRWA.

(b) Structure

i. The Commission shall be governed by an Executive Board (Board) composed of representatives of its members.

ii. The Board shall be the highest authority in the Commission and shall make the relevant policy decisions in accordance with this Agreement.

iii. The Board shall draw up the procedures governing the work of the Commission in accordance with this Agreement.

iv. The Board shall oversee the conduct of the various Committees of the Commission. The said Committees shall periodically report to the Board in accordance with procedures set forth thereby.

v. The Board shall create a Secretariat and appoint a Chair thereof. The Chair and the Secretariat shall conduct the day-to-day operation of the Commission.

(c) Specific Committees

    i. The Commission shall establish the Technical Committees specified below.

    ii. Unless otherwise specified in this Agreement, the Board shall determine the structure and procedures of the Committees.

    iii. The Parties may make submissions to the Committees as deemed necessary.

    iv. The Committees shall establish mechanisms for resolution of disputes arising from the interpretation or implementation of the provisions of this Agreement relating to refugees.

    v. The Committees shall function in accordance with this Agreement, and shall render binding decisions accordingly.

    vi. Refugees shall have the right to appeal decisions affecting them according to mechanisms established by this Agreement and detailed in Annex X.

(d) Status-determination Committee:

    i. The Status-determination Committee shall be responsible for verifying refugee status.

    ii. UNRWA registration shall be considered as rebuttable presumption (prima facie proof) of refugee status.

(e) Compensation Committee:

    i. The Compensation Committee shall be responsible for administering the implementation of the compensation provisions.

    ii. The Committee shall disburse compensation for individual property pursuant to the following modalities: 1. Either a fixed per capita award for property claims below a specified value. This will require the claimant to only prove title, and shall be processed according to a fast-track procedure, or 2. A claims-based award for property claims exceeding a specified value for immovables and other assets. This will require the claimant to prove both title and the value of the losses.

    iii. Annex X shall elaborate the details of the above including, but not limited to, evidentiary issues and the use of UNCCP, "Custodian for Absentees' Property," and UNRWA records, along with any other relevant records.

(f) Host State Remuneration Committee: There shall be remuneration for host states.

(g) Permanent Place of Residence Committee (PPR Committee): The PPR Committee shall,

    i. Develop with all the relevant parties detailed programs regarding the implementation of the PPR options pursuant to Article 7/4 above.

    ii. Assist the applicants in making an informed choice regarding PPR options.

    iii. Receive applications from refugees regarding PPR. The applicants must indicate a number of preferences in accordance with article 7/4 above. The applications shall be received no later than two years after the start of the International Commission's operations. Refugees who do not submit such applications within the two-year period shall lose their refugee status.

    iv. Determine, in accordance with sub-Article (a) above, the PPR of the applicants, taking into account individual preferences and maintenance of family unity. Applicants who do not avail themselves of the Committee's PPR determination shall lose their refugee status.

    v. Provide the applicants with the appropriate technical and legal assistance.

    vi. The PPR of Palestinian refugees shall be realized within 5 years of the start of the International Commission's operations.

(h) Refugeehood Fund Committee: The Refugeehood Fund Committee shall implement Article 7/10 as detailed in Annex X.

(i) Rehabilitation and Development Committee: In accordance with the aims of this Agreement and noting the above PPR programs, the Rehabilitation and Development Committee shall work closely with Palestine, Host Countries and other relevant third countries and parties in pursuing the goal of refugee rehabilitation and community development. This shall include devising programs and plans to provide the former refugees with opportunities for personal and communal development, housing, education, healthcare, re-training and other needs. This shall be integrated in the general development plans for the region.

12. The International Fund

(a) An International Fund (the Fund) shall be established to receive contributions outlined in this Article and additional contributions from the international community. The Fund shall disburse monies to the Commission to enable it to carry out its functions. The Fund shall audit the Commission's work.

(b) The structure, composition and operation of the Fund are set forth in Annex X.

13. UNRWA

(a) UNRWA should be phased out in each country in which it operates, based on the end of refugee status in that country.

(b) UNRWA should cease to exist five years after the start of the Commission's operations. The Commission shall draw up a plan for the phasing out of UNRWA and shall facilitate the transfer of UNRWA functions to host states.

14. Reconciliation Programs

(a) The Parties will encourage and promote the development of cooperation between their relevant institutions and civil societies in creating forums for exchanging historical narratives and enhancing mutual understanding regarding the past.

(b) The Parties shall encourage and facilitate exchanges in order to disseminate a richer appreciation of these respective narratives, in the fields of formal and informal education, by providing conditions for direct contacts between schools, educational institutions, and civil society.

(c) The Parties may consider cross-community cultural programs in order to promote the goals of conciliation in relation to their respective histories.

(d) These programs may include developing appropriate ways of commemorating those villages and communities that existed prior to 1949.

Article 8—Israeli-Palestinian Cooperation Committee (IPCC)

1. The Parties shall establish an Israeli-Palestinian Cooperation Committee immediately upon the entry into force of this agreement. The IPCC shall be a ministerial-level body with ministerial-level Co-Chairs.

2. The IPCC shall develop and assist in the implementation of policies for cooperation in areas of common interest including, but not limited to, infrastructure needs, sustainable development and environmental issues, cross-border municipal cooperation, border area industrial parks, exchange programs, human resource development, sports and youth, science, agriculture and culture.

3. The IPCC shall strive to broaden the spheres and scope of cooperation between the Parties.

Article 9—Designated Road Use Arrangements

1. The following arrangements for Israeli civilian use will apply to the designated roads in Palestine as detailed in Map X (Road 443, Jerusalem to Tiberias via Jordan Valley, and Jerusalem –Ein Gedi).

2. These arrangements shall not prejudice Palestinian jurisdiction over these roads, including PSF patrols.

3. The procedures for designated road use arrangements will be further detailed in Annex X.

4. Israelis may be granted permits for use of designated roads. Proof of authorization may be presented at entry points to the designated roads. The sides will review options for establishing a road use system based on smart card technology.

5. The designated roads will be patrolled by the MF at all times. The MF will establish with the states of Israel and Palestine agreed arrangements for cooperation in emergency medical evacuation of Israelis.

6. In the event of any incidents involving Israeli citizens and requiring criminal or legal proceedings, there will be full cooperation between the Israeli and Palestinian authorities according to arrangements to be agreed upon as part of the legal cooperation between the two states. The Parties may call on the IVG to assist in this respect.

7. Israelis shall not use the designated roads as a means of entering Palestine without the relevant documentation and authorization.

8. In the event of regional peace, arrangements for Palestinian civilian use of designated roads in Israel shall be agreed and come into effect.

Article 10—Sites of Religious Significance

1. The Parties shall establish special arrangements to guarantee access to agreed sites of religious significance, as will be detailed in Annex X. These arrangements will apply, inter alia, to the Tomb of the Patriarchs in Hebron and Rachel's Tomb in Bethlehem, and Nabi Samuel.

2. Access to and from the sites will be by way of designated shuttle facilities from the relevant border crossing to the sites.

3. The Parties shall agree on requirements and procedures for granting licenses to authorized private shuttle operators.
4. The shuttles and passengers will be subject to MF inspection.
5. The shuttles will be escorted on their route between the border crossing and the sites by the MF.
6. The shuttles shall be under the traffic regulations and jurisdiction of the Party in whose territory they are traveling.
7. Arrangements for access to the sites on special days and holidays are detailed in Annex X.
8. The Palestinian Tourist Police and the MF will be present at these sites.
9. The Parties shall establish a joint body for the religious administration of these sites.
10. In the event of any incidents involving Israeli citizens and requiring criminal or legal proceedings, there will be full cooperation between the Israeli and Palestinian authorities according to arrangements to be agreed upon. The Parties may call on the IVG to assist in this respect.
11. Israelis shall not use the shuttles as a means of entering Palestine without the relevant documentation and authorization.
12. The Parties shall protect and preserve the sites of religious significance listed in Annex X and shall facilitate visitation to the cemeteries listed in Annex X.

Article 11—Border Regime

1. There shall be a border regime between the two states, with movement between them subject to the domestic legal requirements of each and to the provisions of this Agreement as detailed in Annex X.
2. Movement across the border shall only be through designated border crossings.

3. Procedures in border crossings shall be designed to facilitate strong trade and economic ties, including labor movement between the Parties.
4. Each Party shall each, in its respective territory, take the measures it deems necessary to ensure that no persons, vehicles, or goods enter the territory of the other illegally.
5. Special border arrangements in Jerusalem shall be in accordance with Article 6 above.

Article 12—Water: still to be completed

Article 13—Economic Relations: still to be completed

Article 14—Legal Cooperation: still to be completed

Article 15—Palestinian Prisoners and Detainees
1. In the context of this Permanent Status Agreement between Israel and Palestine, the end of conflict, cessation of all violence, and the robust security arrangements set forth in this Agreement, all the Palestinian and Arab prisoners detained in the framework of the Israeli-Palestinian conflict prior to the date of signature of this Agreement, DD/MM/2003, shall be released in accordance with the categories set forth below and detailed in Annex X.
    (a) Category A: all persons imprisoned prior to the start of the implementation of the Declaration of Principles on May 4, 1994, administrative detainees, and minors, as well as women, and prisoners in ill health shall be released immediately upon the entry into force of this Agreement.
    (b) Category B: all persons imprisoned after May 4, 1994 and prior to the signature of this Agreement shall be released no later than eighteen months from the entry into force of this Agreement,

except those specified in Category C.

(c) Category C: Exceptional cases—persons whose names are set forth in Annex X—shall be released in thirty months at the end of the full implementation of the territorial aspects of this Agreement set forth in Article 5/7/v.

Article 16—Dispute Settlement Mechanism

1. Disputes related to the interpretation or application of this Agreement shall be resolved by negotiations within a bilateral framework to be convened by the High Steering Committee.

2. If a dispute is not settled promptly by the above, either Party may submit it to mediation and conciliation by the IVG mechanism in accordance with Article 3.

3. Disputes which cannot be settled by bilateral negotiation and/or the IVG mechanism shall be settled by a mechanism of conciliation to be agreed upon by the Parties.

4. Disputes which have not been resolved by the above may be submitted by either Party to an arbitration panel. Each Party shall nominate one member of the three-member arbitration panel. The Parties shall select a third arbiter from the agreed list of arbiters set forth in Annex X either by consensus or, in the case of disagreement, by rotation.

Article 17—Final Clauses

Including a final clause providing for a UNSCR/UNGAR resolution endorsing the agreement and superceding the previous UN resolutions.

The English version of this text will be considered authoritative.

3. The Immediate Reaction

Ariel Sharon denounced the Geneva Accord as "subversive," and two cabinet ministers called the Israeli negotiators "traitors ... a crime punishable by death." Some of the right-wing denunciations trumpeted the already-obvious flaw that the negotiators did not represent the Israeli state and had no right to make agreements in its name. But neither Israeli nor Palestinian negotiators claimed to be official representatives of the governments of their countries —they were preparing a document that *could* be the final resolution of the conflict.

Polls still showed substantial support for the Geneva Accords in Israel, a support that grew when, in the months after the signing, several million copies of the Accord were mailed to Israeli citizens.

The mere existence of the unofficial Accord had a quick and dramatic impact on internal Israeli politics. Sharon was put on the defensive; he had to explain why the Occupation continued to be necessary. His position was rescued in part, however, by the fact that the Accord was received with mixed reactions even from the opposition Labor Party. On the one hand, the peace-oriented wing of the Labor Party embraced and celebrated the Accord. Amram Mitzna, Labor's candidate for Prime Minister in the 2003 election, gave public speeches on its behalf. There was no doubt that it represented the position that he would have supported had he been elected.

Yet Ehud Barak denounced the Accord, largely on the grounds that he did not believe it made sense to trust the Palestinians to the degree that the document proposed. Peace-oriented observers noted the difficulty the Accord raised for Barak, who had just explained the failure of Camp David as a manifestation of the "fact" that there was "no partner for peace." If, on the other hand, the Accord represented a serious decision on the part of the leadership of the Palestinian Authority to make serious concessions for peace, then the problem at Camp David may not have been the absence of a partner as much as the absence of skill and intention from Barak himself. To counter that reading of the history and its critique of him personally, peace advocates argued, Barak was now defensively positioning himself against the Accord.

But was there support for the Accord on the Palestinian side? According to accounts given by the Palestinian negotiators, every major part of the agreement had been discussed by the top leadership, including Arafat himself, at each stage in the negotiations, and the final agreement reflected what he and other top Palestinian Authority figures would agree to in a final resolution of the conflict. I stress:

"would agree to in a final resolution of the conflict"; that did not make it an opening Palestinian negotiating posture or even a position they would adopt on a tit-for-tat basis prior to a final resolution.

Even so, why didn't Arafat himself publicly endorse the Accord or have the Authority endorse it? The Palestinian negotiators explained that Arafat had made it fully clear that if the Israeli government would agree to the Accord, so would the Authority. But, Arafat has argued, official Palestinian government institutions cannot today endorse the Accord because if they do the Israelis will argue in any future negotiations that the Accord represents the *opening* position of the Palestinians—and the Israelis will then present their opening position as one calling for retention by Israel of the territories, and on that basis ask for compromises between the two positions. From the standpoint of the Palestinian Authority, the Geneva Accord represents a final compromise, not an opening position, and so the PA is not willing to officially endorse it.

Doesn't that mean that both sides are equally distant from the Geneva Accord? No. There is no doubt that the PA would immediately accept any initiative by the international community that made the Geneva Accord the foundation for negotiations for a final settlement, while the Israeli government would not. In April of 2004 there are indications the

PA may publicly endorse the Accord. Does that fact itself speak to the unfairness of the agreement, its one-sided support for the needs of the Palestinian people over the needs of Israel? Not at all. As we'll see in the next sections, there have been substantial arguments brought against the Geneva Accord by partisans on both sides. The willingness of the PA to embrace the Accord as a foundation for negotiations, should that be proposed by Israel or the United States, is based on the parties' present relative levels of desperation, not an assessment that the deal favors their interests over Israel. In fact, as we shall see below, many Palestinians believe that giving up of the Right of Return was a huge and, for some, unacceptable compromise built into the Geneva document.

The positive response of the international community was immediate, reflected in a broadly representative statement printed in the *International Herald Tribune* endorsing both the Geneva Accord and a declaration of principles along similar lines being circulated by Ami Ayalon, the former head of Israel's Shin Bet security service and Sari Nusseibeh, president of Al Quds University, Jerusalem.

This statement read in part:

We believe that the best way to move forward is to address at the outset, not at the end of an incremental process, all the basic principles of a fair and lasting solution. Postponing the final outcome makes any progress hostage to extremists on both sides. A process must be devised to give practical and political expression to the heartfelt desire of clear majorities on both sides to end this conflict once and for all.

The Geneva and People's Voice initiatives both reflect that public opinion and can help give it new momentum. On the Israeli side, they can help undo the myths that have taken hold since the collapse of the peace process and onset of violence: that the Palestinian people are not prepared to accept a two-state solution and Israel's right to exist as a Jewish state. On the Palestinian side, they can offer an alternative to the current mindset that sees in violence the only possible means of ending the Occupation. They send a powerful signal that an alternative to the current situation exists. They have the potential to transform the domestic political dynamics on both sides.

International support will be crucial to translate these endeavors into a concrete mechanism to bring about a lasting peace. The international players most relevant for this purpose—the "quartet" composed of the United States, the EU, Russia, and the UN, and the members of the Arab League—should wholeheartedly back these initiatives. They should urge both the Israeli government and the Palestinian Authority to be guided by the outcomes most of their peoples want. And they should make clear their own willingness to lend all the political, economic, and military support needed to help implement a comprehensive peace agreement.

The Israeli and Palestinian peoples, by making clear their belief in the Geneva and People's Voice initiatives, can help turn the principles embodied in them into reality. You can count on our support in this endeavor."

Signed by: Marti Ahtisaari, former president, Finland; **Ali Alatas,** former foreign minister, Indonesia; **George Alleyne,** former director, Pan American Health Organization; **Oscar Arias Sánchez,** former president, Costa Rica; **Lloyd Axworthy,** former foreign minister, Canada; **Alexander Bessmertnykh,** former foreign minister, U.S.S.R.; **Carl Bildt,** former prime minister, Sweden; **Boutros Boutros-Ghali,** former secretary general, UN; **Lakhdar Brahimi,** former foreign minister, Algeria; **Fernando Henrique Cardoso,** former president, Brazil; **Ingvar Carlsson,** former prime minister, Sweden; **Lord Carrington,** former foreign secretary, U.K., former secretary general, NATO; **Jorge Castañeda,** former foreign minister, Mexico; **Claude Cheysson,** former foreign minister, France; **Jacques Delors,** former president, EC; **Jiri Dienstbier,** former foreign minister, Czechoslovakia; **Ruth Dreifuss,** former president, Switzerland; **Uffe Ellemann-Jensen,** former foreign minister, Denmark; **Gareth Evans,** former foreign minister, Australia; **Mark Eyskens,** former prime minister, Belgium; **José Maria Figueres,**

former president, Costa Rica; **Malcolm Fraser,** former prime minister, Australia; **Hans-Dietrich Genscher,** former foreign minister, Germany; **Bronislaw Geremek,** former foreign minister, Poland; **Mikhail Gorbachev,** former president, U.S.S.R.; **I. K. Gujral,** former prime minister, India; **Bob Hawke,** former prime minister, Australia; **Bill Hayden,** former governor-general, former foreign minister, Australia; **Raffi K. Hovannisian,** former foreign minister, Armenia; **F. W. de Klerk,** former president, South Africa; **Wim Kok,** former prime minister, Netherlands; **Masahiko Komura,** former foreign minister, Japan; **Budimir Loncar,** former foreign minister, Yugoslavia; **Barbara McDougall,** former secretary of state for external affairs, Canada; **Gianni de Michelis,** former foreign minister, Italy; **Boyko Noev,** former defense minister, Bulgaria; **Sadako Ogata,** former UN High Commissioner for Refugees; **Lord David Owen,** former foreign secretary, U.K.; **Surin Pitsuwan,** former foreign minister, Thailand; **Augusto Ramírez Ocampo,** former foreign minister, Colombia; **Fidel Ramos,** former president, Philippines; **J. J. Rawlings,** former president, Ghana; **Mary Robinson,** former president, Ireland; **Michel Rocard,** former prime minister, France; **Nafis Sadik,** former executive director, UN Population Fund; **Salim Ahmed Salim,** former secretary-general, OAU; **Cornelio Sommaruga,** former president, International Committee of the Red Cross; **Kalevi Sorsa,** former prime minister, Finland; **Eduardo**

Stein, former foreign minister, Guatemala; **Pär Stenbäck,** former foreign minister, Finland; **Max van der Stoel,** former foreign minister, Netherlands; **Thorvald Stoltenberg,** former foreign minister, Norway; **Hanna Suchocka,** former prime minister, Poland; **Alex Sceberras Trigona,** former foreign minister, Malta; **George Vassiliou,** former president, Cyprus; **Hubert Védrine,** former foreign minister, France; **Franz Vranitzky,** former federal chancellor, Austria; **Ernesto Zedillo,** former president, Mexico.

Dozens of testimonies of support came from current government leaders around the globe. Unfortunately, while U.S. Secretary of State Colin Powell welcomed the Geneva Accord, there was not an equivalent welcoming or endorsement by President Bush. The U.S. government took the position of many in the pro-Sharon forces in the U.S. led by AIPAC, the American Israel Political Affairs Committee—that this agreement had no particular or unique significance, given that it did not represent the positions of the respective governments. Instead of calling upon the governments to begin final status negotiations based on the Geneva Accord, the Administration made abstract references to hopes that the odyssey along its own Road Map for peace would be restarted.

The major problem with the Administration's Road Map, however, is that it provides no incentive for completion because it does not specify where the map is leading. It risks being a self-serving document set up to make its architects look honorable while actually sabotaging its ostensible goal. Parties are supposed to take steps along an imaginary road, but the final destination and outcome are left to a later time to be defined. The Geneva Accord provided the missing link: a specific picture of what the destination for a Road Map could be. Had the Administration embraced that destination, its Road Map might have been revived. Or even had the Administration said that it recognized that final-status negotiations should begin immediately, using the Geneva Accord as its foundation, it would have been able to revive hope and begin a serious process. But it didn't serve the purposes of Bush, Dick Cheney, and their confederates to begin a serious peace process—purposes which always placed narrow political ambitions ahead of honest brokering in the international arena.

There is nothing in the Geneva Accord that fundamentally challenges the right-wing worldview that shapes the Administration's perspective on the U.S. role among nations. Peace in the Middle East would not necessarily weaken and might arguably strengthen the effectuality of the United States in its goal to dominate the rest of the Middle East. In fact, it might be contended that a peace made possible through something like a Geneva Accord would give the

United States a stronger hand in its program to represent itself as a force for democratic reconstruction of the world, thereby giving it more support in the Arab world and greater credibility should it seek to extend its imperial control by invading Syria, Iran, or another rogue state. An intelligent imperialist might argue that the Accord should be embraced on those grounds alone (not that I support this logic).

Political commentators in the United States had no problem understanding why the Administration had not embraced the Geneva Accord. From the standpoint of the current dynamics in American politics, there is no organized force (outside perhaps the Tikkun Community and its allies) that is seeking to make support for the Geneva Accord a serious factor in how people assess candidates for public office. On the other hand, there is a powerful set of right-wing PACs both in the Jewish and fundamentalist Christian milieus that are determined to punish any candidate for public office who publicly challenges the policies of the present Israeli government. The Bush Administration has hopes of winning significant right-wing Jewish support in states where the presidential election might be close: Florida, Pennsylvania, Michigan, Illinois, and, under certain circumstances, New York and California. To take a stance in opposition to Israel in 2004 would significantly weaken Bush's chances of winning close votes. Moreover, Arab-

American voters, who are far less organized politically, may have already been lost to the Bush camp as a result of the Administration's post 9/11 suppression of civil liberties which has had a disproportionate impact on Muslims who are often treated as *a priori* suspects because they share a religion with the fundamentalists behind the 9/11 attack.

The Democrats are not immune to similar strategic reasoning. That accounts for their failure to enthusiastically embrace or even publicly discuss the Accord. Democrats believe that Jewish voters who are liberal on a wide variety of topics but right-wing on the issue of Israel might defect from them should their nominee become identified with a program perceived as critical of the Israeli government.

A short while before the Geneva Accord was released, Democratic Presidential candidate Howard Dean made a statement calling for a more "even-handed" policy by the United States if it hoped to play the role of "honest broker" in the Middle East. Dean was immediately attacked in a public letter signed by dozens of liberal Democratic Congresspeople led by the Minority Leader of the House of Representatives, Nancy Pelosi. Dean was, in effect, castigated for seeming to challenge the special relationship between the United States and Israel. He backed down immediately, though later commentators have suggested that the increasingly rough treatment he received by the media in the months immediately preceding the Iowa caucuses may have been related to his having shown himself to be "non-presidential" by daring to cross this shared bipartisan perspective that the United States should rubberstamp the policies of the State of Israel.

In any event, none of the Democrats running for the nomination were willing to make support for a peace perspective a central part of their campaign, much less even to discuss the Geneva Accord or any of the other proposals emanating from the Israeli peace movement. Senators John Kerry and John Edwards have done their best to assure the leaders of the Jewish community that they stand solidly behind Israel and have not in any way recommended that backing the Israeli peace movement is part of their agenda. Yet I believe it should be, as this would in fact represent true support for Israel at a critical historical moment.

The dynamics of Diaspora life often push non-Israeli Jews to support the most extreme elements in Israel. Many American Jews feel guilty at not having personally taken the risks of the Israelis and so, instead of exercising their critical faculties and asking themselves, "What might best help create peace in Israel?" they tell themselves, "We have no right to substitute our own judgments for that of the Israeli people and its democratically elected government."

So, as expected, liberal forces in the American Jewish

community have been tepid and constrained in their response to the Geneva Accord. Most found reason to not comment at all or to give it a weak-hearted endorsement and then move on to other topics. The most significant of the liberal forces, the Reform Movement of Judaism, is undergoing an internal battle around this and other Israel-related issues. There are many genuinely peace-and-justice-oriented people in the Reform movement (indeed, in every branch and strand of Judaism), but they are often put on the defensive by others who are convinced that Israel's security cannot be entrusted to any peace forces and that it is only the Ariel Sharons who will actually be able to keep Israel strong enough to survive.

Rather than conduct that argument in a clear and explicit way and hence allow the members of the Reform movement to vote in a nationwide referendum on how the Reform movement should position itself on Israel-related questions, the national leadership has feared splitting its constituency along political/ideological lines and chosen instead to take a path that avoids the most controversial and cutting-edge issues. Hence, while it has welcomed Geneva, it has chosen not to use its considerable educational and political resources to back the actual Accord.

In the mainstream world of the federations that control the bulk of the money in the Jewish world and their associated community relations organizations, there has been little enthusiasm for the Geneva Accord. The major Jewish institutions are structured around a mind-set portraying Israel as eternally and irrevocably endangered by the Palestinian people, and this positioning inspires substantial donations by playing directly on those fears. To suddenly encourage (or even allow) its donors to recognize that a set of options for safety and security now exist and could be implemented were Israel to enthusiastically embrace it would be to attempt to reverse at least fifty years of institutional direction and leadership.

In the Palestinian world outside of Palestine, the same kind of dynamics hold sway. Guilt at not having been on the front lines of the struggle, combined with self-reproach at "making it" in the United States, leads many Palestinian Americans to side with the most extreme rejectionist elements in Palestine. As a result, instead of rejoicing at the publication of the Geneva Accord, many embraced radical critiques that claim that the Accord has "sold out" Palestinian interests by agreeing to abandon the Right of Return (and in other ways which we shall consider below).

The one other forum by which the Geneva Accord might have been thrust into the limelight of the American media, and from there into the attention of the public, would have been its embrace by the anti-war movement. The force that

73

mobilized millions of people into the streets in opposition to the war in Iraq could have played a major role in making the Geneva Accord a household concept in the United States and pushing the media to address it.

Unfortunately, the two major anti-war coalitions, the A.N.S.W.E.R. coalition and United for Peace and Justice, are dominated by those who identify with the rejectionist elements in the American Palestinian community. For the A.N.S.W.E.R. coalition, this was a no-brainer: their leadership has consistently been hostile to the very existence of the State of Israel. When I challenged the national spokesperson of A.N.S.W.E.R. (on a live radio show) to affirm the right of the Jewish people to national self-determination in their ancient homeland, his response was that this was "a matter for the people of the region to decide." Of course, such an answer is tantamount to "no" because the people of the region have deep-seated animosities to the Jewish people. And it makes no sense, because if national self-determination were the prerogative of the people of the region to decide, African Americans would have never won the right to vote in the American South.

For United for Peace and Justice (UFPJ), the tendency to support the anti-accomodationist wing of the Palestinian world is less a matter of deep-seated conviction than a reflection of unimaginative leadership combined with an inability to pursue clear thinking or strategy in a coherent way. So, for example, the old-New Left tendencies to eschew powerful leadership, avoid ideological debate, and give knee-jerk support to whomever is determined to be "the most oppressed," without asking oneself whether those "most oppressed" actually have the best ideas about how to end the oppression—all these combine to tilt UFPJ toward a lack of serious interest in tying itself to the Geneva Accord.

Who that leaves actively and publicly backing the Geneva Accord is my own Tikkun Community, a national interfaith organization that supports a "progressive middle path" that is both pro-Israel and pro-Palestine, as well as Americans for Peace Now, Brit Tzedeck ve Shalom, The Israel Policy Forum, and Meretz USA. Through different strategies, all of these organizations are reaching out to governmental representatives both in the United States and in Israel, as well as intellectuals, students, the media, independent institutions, and other opinion shapers in an effort to influence U.S. policy in the Middle East.

4. Arguments against the Geneva Accord from those who think it unfairly favors the Palestinians

The ink was barely dry, and some parts not yet filled in, when the Right began its attacks. Yossi Klein Halevi and Michael B. Oren, both Fellows at the right-wing think tank The Shalem Center, labeled the enterprise a "fantasy" in the virulently anti-Palestinian *New Republic* magazine. Objections One to Ten below are based on their arguments in *The New Republic,* sometimes quoting directly.

Objection One

Although the sponsors of the Geneva Accord "insist that the Accord is merely a proposal by private citizens, the text is presented as a 'permanent-status agreement' between Israel and the Palestinian Liberation Organization (PLO), complete with highly detailed articles and color-coded maps."

Response

The implication here is that it is inappropriate for mere citizens to engage in developing detailed plans of what a solution to the Occupation might look like. This is a task for governments.

Yes, it would be great if governments engaged in this activity. But what if they don't and war continues? The answer has been provided by a global movement for "citizens' diplomacy." Ordinary people themselves come up with plans for an accommodation, and eventually some of these ideas manage to capture public attention and support and then are foisted onto governments that have acted contrary to the peaceful aspirations of their own populace. Often this kind of development is necessary when one or other side reports that "there is nobody to negotiate with" because of the other side's alleged intransigence. When an agreement gets written by ordinary citizens, it shows that there are people to talk to, people who really want peace, and that in itself plays a critical role in the evolution of dialogue; it sparks a breakthrough in consciousness which can lead more people on one side or the other to start to push for a peace that is really possible and then elect governments that will support that push. Can you give an analogous example here? Vietnam War?

Objection Two

"The centrist Israeli majority supports establishing a Palestinian state, but only after the Palestinians have ended terrorism, reformed their government, and renounced their insistence on returning Palestinian refugees to Israel. The

77

Accord, though, ignores even those minimal expectations. Instead, it would grant the Palestinians a state while they wage a terrorist war, legitimize and even strengthen Yasser Arafat's rule, and force Israel to accept the principle of repatriating refugees. In addition, it undermines the global war on terrorism and would threaten any future compromise in the region."

Response

Let's take the claim that the "Israeli majority supports establishing a Palestinian state, but only after the Palestinians ..." There couldn't be a more empty claim. If someone said that "the Palestinian majority supports living in peace with Israel, but only after Israel purges itself of its tendency to dominate the Palestinian people through force and violence, renounces its insistence on giving Jews a Right of Return to the land of Israel, and reforms its corrupt economic practices, which distribute state revenues in a way that systematically discriminates against Israeli Arabs," you'd hardly claim that this was an indication of openness to anything.

The demand that the Palestinians end terrorism before Israel signs the Geneva Accord and allows the Palestinians to establish a state has no more legitimacy than if the Palestinians were to say that they demand Israel withdraw from the Occupied Territories and give up their advanced weaponry before they will sign the Geneva Accord.

There were people in the United States who wanted to make this same demand in regard to Vietnam—they claimed that the United States couldn't get out of Vietnam until the North Vietnamese and National Liberation Front ended its hostilities. Had the United States continued to take that position, Americans would still be fighting the Vietnam War.

What makes the demand plausible to Israelis is that they imagine that they have the military strength to get away with it. If the military balance of power were different and more equal, Israelis would quickly agree that it is in their interests to end the Occupation, and the Geneva Accord would be embraced as a good deal for Israel.

Let's look now at the specifics. On the surface, it might seem reasonable to want the Palestinian people to stop waging a terrorist war. The terror is self-destructive for the Palestinian people and is not the most effective political strategy—apart from the deeper objection that it is, in my view, fundamentally immoral to direct assaults against innocent civilians.

On the other hand, whenever superior military forces occupy a civilian population which has no army of its own, terrorist tactics become one of the few ways that the occupied populations have figured out how to wage war to free themselves from the occupiers. And it has worked.

Moreover, occupation is almost always a terrorist occupation itself. As noted above, the Israeli human rights organization B'tselem provides detailed documentation of the daily violent assault on innocent Palestinian civilians by the Israeli Defense Forces—so one need not rely on conjecture. Ending terrorism is not a one-sided imperative.

Another problem with this demand is that it's impossible for the Palestinian Authority to meet it, and Israel knows this. The Authority faces a challenge from a significant force of Islamic fundamentalists who do not recognize the legitimacy of the secular government. In the period before the Intifada, the PA was beginning to develop might that could eventually have given it the power to suppress the military wing of this Islamic fundamentalist movement. But during Intifada II the Israeli leaders, responding to attacks from Hamas and the Islamic Jihad, responded not by destroying those movements but by retaliating against the Authority! Now, given that Hamas and Islamic Jihad already wanted to replace the Palestinian Authority by its own constabulary, this kind of retaliation, ostensibly a deterrent against terrorism, was in fact an incentive for future acts of terror, since the terrorists would be directly rewarded by IDF assaults against their enemy, the PA. The PA would be sufficiently weakened so that it was in no position to arrest terrorists or destroy the terrorist/suicide-bombing movement. All the PA can really do is to issue statements condemning acts of terror, which it regularly does.

Why would the Ariel Sharon government act in this obviously irrational way? Assume, as I do, that Ariel Sharon and those surrounding him are not stupid, and then you have to assume next that his government actively sought the weakening of the Palestinian Authority to such an extent that it would not be able to provide a counter-weight to Hamas. In that case, of course, Sharon would be able to do what he has actually done: claim that since the Palestinian Authority can't keep the terrorism in check, there is "nobody with whom to negotiate."

Still, you might respond, "Why can't the Palestinian Authority mobilize popular support to oppose the violence, assuming its claims to represent the majority of people in the West Bank are true, and the majority opposes violence?"

There are two reasons why this is extremely difficult:

In order to mobilize a mass movement to oppose violence, the PA would have to be able to make a plausible case that once the violence stopped, the Israeli population would in fact act to end the Occupation and establish the basis for a Palestinian state. However, in the period between 1993–2000, when violence was at a very low level, the Israeli population did not at all act to end the Occupation, but in fact expanded the number of settlers in the West Bank and Gaza and increased the number of roadblocks, even though Israel had signed the Oslo Accord promising to do exactly the opposite. Unless the Israeli government were to make some dramatic gesture to inspire the Palestinian people to believe that they were facing a different situation (e.g. by publicly embracing the Geneva Accord and beginning to dismantle the most provocative settlements like those in Hebron and Kiryat Arba), most Palestinians would feel that their nonviolence was only a gift to the Israeli occupiers, who would have every intention of maintaining the Occupation.

There are some Islamic fundamentalist and Jewish fundamentalist groups who do not want the agreement to succeed. They each believe that they have been given the land of Israel as their eternal inheritance and to share it with the other side would be to violate God's will. These people are unlikely to be much influenced by a popular nonviolent movement. And if they know that they can disrupt a peace process by acting violently, they will. The surest way to disempower those people is to make it clear both in words and in deeds that they will *not* be able to stop peace by their acts of violence, rather than to give them the impression that all they need do is kill some people on the other side to disrupt the process and intensify the conflict.

Objection Three

"Most Israelis have long since lost any faith in the willingness of Arafat's regime to uphold any agreement with Israel. Under Oslo, the Palestinian Authority (P.A.) pledged to refrain from incitement, actively combat terrorism, limit the weaponry in its arsenal, and peacefully resolve all disputes with Israel. Instead, it has educated a generation of Palestinian youth to revere suicide bombers, actively abetted terrorism, smuggled in tens of thousands of illegal weapons, and responded to Israel's peace offers with a war that has killed or wounded thousands on both sides."

Response

It is true that most Israelis have lost faith in the willingness of Arafat's regime to uphold any agreement with Israel. Yet this one-sided reading of what happened since the signing of the Oslo Accord is the reason why that loss of faith has occurred. Israelis are totally unable to grasp their own responsibility for the decline of faith among Palestinians about Oslo and hence Palestinian unwillingness to use military force to stop the terrorists among them who, while determined to undermine the agreement, were also at least resisting the Occupation and upholding community pride.

If Israelis would look at the history, they'd realize that

the first significant break after Oslo occurred when a Jewish fundamentalist extremist entered the Mosque at the Cave of the Patriarchs in Hebron and killed twenty-nine Muslims at prayer. Israelis would recognize that it was the fundamentalists in the Jewish camp who slowed the process of withdrawal from the West Bank under Israeli Prime Minister Yitzhak Rabin by declaring him a traitor for signing Oslo, proceeding to instigate disloyalty among religious Jews in the IDF, engaging in acts of civil disobedience, and engendering a climate of violence so hate-filled that one of the more inflamed religious fundamentalists murdered Rabin. Nor will Israelis note that one of the first things authorized by Shimon Peres after taking office following the death of Rabin was to assassinate a Hamas terrorist, which in turn incited Hamas bus-bombings just before the elections in 1996, which in turn led to the election of a two-year Likud government unwilling to implement Oslo. The idea that somehow the responsibility for the failure of Oslo could one-sidedly be put on Palestinians intentionally obscures these realities. It allows the pro-Sharon side to bathe in the story of Jewish-self-righteousness while ignoring the more complex and ethically muddled reality.

Objection Four

"Not only does Geneva ignore the collapse of Palestinian credibility, it denies Israel the means to defend itself. While even Oslo gave Israeli security forces the right of hot pursuit against terrorists, Geneva would place Israel's security in the hands of a multinational force composed of contingents from the 'United States, the Russian Federation, the European Union, the UN, and other parties.' The force would be charged with monitoring Palestinian compliance with the Accord, patrolling borders, and preventing terrorist attacks and arms smuggling. Israel and Palestine would have the right to assent to the force, but the Accord is unclear on whether the two parties can veto the countries providing monitors. Consequently, given international pressure on Israel, can anyone imagine it being able to veto the participation of, say, France and Belgium?"

Response

The reference here to France and Belgium is presumably to the shared consensus in Israel that these states can't be trusted (precisely because they have been publicly critical of various human-rights violations committed by the Sharon government). The Right points to the UN resolution condemning "Zionism as racism" as proof that the countries of the world cannot be counted on as impartial in any respect. It is certainly true that that resolution was itself a racist move, because it gave special attention to the wrongs being committed by the Israeli government and sought to make those qualitatively different from equal or worse wrongs being committed by other human-rights-denying countries at the time (the UN did subsequently vote to revoke that resolution). Some right-wingers argue that these kinds of actions—e.g. the original resolution—permanently discredit the UN. But if so, that puts Israel into exactly the cul-de-sac in which the Right wishes it to be: alone against the world, with the United States as an occasional and not-to-be-counted-on ally.

This is also precisely how many Israelis and Jews perceive the world. Acting from an inflated, victim-as-revenger paranoid assumption, Israelis and right-wing Jews actually create a world that roughly resembles the world they fear. This is self-fulfilling prophecy in the worst possible sense. Most people in the world do not have a legacy of hate against Jews. Unlike the Christian West, most people on the planet do not even have Jews as part of their symbolic legacy. Their anger at Israeli behavior comes from two significant, contemporary sources:

1. The actual behavior of the State of Israel about which they know far more than they do about other societies, in

part because the West, which dominates international media, has such a fascination with Israel that it places a disproportionate amount of media attention on what is happening there. That attention includes a special attachment that Western Christians have to the Holy Land; it is not only *not* a reflection of negative intentions, it has played a role in making the United States receptive to giving Israel significantly more foreign aid than it does any other country on the planet. The increased attention, however, simultaneously puts more focus on the defects of Israeli society. And it is those defects, particularly the acts of one of the most powerful armies in the world as it imposes an occupation on a mostly unarmed civilian population, that generates anger at Israel in particular and at Jews who are seen as supporting Israel uncritically. It is not a trenchant, millennia-old anti-Semitism.

2. Some of the anger directed at Israel is deflected outrage at the United States and its role in the world. The United States, with five percent of the world's population, owns twenty-five percent of the world's wealth. Its peremptory tactics to shape the global economy have earned it its own fair level of resentment and anger. Yet precisely because of its power, which can manifest in ways that are unpredictable and pervasive on economic, political, and cultural levels, many of those most piqued at the United States are also

fearful of expressing their rage in ways that might endanger themselves. Israel is seen as a lap-dog surrogate of American power, in part because for the past thirty years the United States has systematically blocked UN resolutions that sought to end the Occupation of the West Bank and Gaza, in part because Israel has shown its loyalty to the United States by backing some of America's foreign policy moves that have received little or no support from any other country in the world. So Israel becomes a perfect target for letting out anger at the U.S.

Yet that anger could be significantly mitigated were Israel to adopt an approach of compassion for the Palestinian people and contrition for the way it has violated their human rights. A major first step would be the act of embracing the Geneva Accord. The enmity that other countries feel towards Israel could be transformed were Israel to act in a transparently generous and open-hearted way toward the Palestinians. On the other hand, to the extent that the Israelis continue to reject proposals like the Geneva Accord that could actually resolve the conflict and do so on the grounds that they can't trust the rest of the world, they end up (see above) creating the very reality that they so much fear. This sad dynamic has become an addictive product of the Jews' constant reinvention and reinvocation of their history of oppression. It should make us all the more committed to compassionately helping Israelis get out of a self-destructive way of thinking about their own situation. I emphasize that the peoples of the world have themselves to blame for allowing Jews to have been so mistreated for so many centuries that Jews finally became traumatized and incapable of acting in their own interests, so the world should act firmly but compassionately toward Israel as it seeks to end Israel's abusive treatment of the Palestinians. The world should ally itself with those Jews inside Israel and in the Diaspora who have been privileged to overcome the trauma sufficiently to recognize that Jewish self-interest is tied to the well-being of the Palestinian people in particular, as well as to the elimination of poverty.

Objection Five

"Israel's experience with such multinational forces is hardly encouraging. Beginning in 1949, border disputes were supposed to be resolved by joint Arab-Israeli committees under the UN's aegis. But these committees proved powerless to prevent terrorist incursions into Israel, and their failure helped precipitate the 1956 Sinai War. UN peacekeeping forces placed in Sinai after that conflict were summarily evicted by Egypt in May 1967, triggering the Six Day War. More recently, UN observer forces in Lebanon have failed to prevent Hezbollah attacks against Israel and have even been implicated in the kidnapping of Israeli soldiers. (Israel's history does offer two examples of successful international peacekeeping: on the Golan Heights after the 1973 War and in Sinai after the Israeli-Egyptian peace treaty in 1979; in both cases, though, success has depended on the Syrian and Egyptian determination to maintain a quiet border.) Yet the Geneva Accord would resurrect the failed 1949 model of joint committees and entrust Israel's security to international peacekeepers."

Response

This kind of detail has to be worked out to the satisfaction of Israel. I agree that international peacekeepers should not be removable by decision of one of the parties and that they must be empowered with the capacity to use force if necessary to stop acts of aggression or terror and the responsibility to do so. To the extent that the practical application of this needs to be further delineated, it can and would be by the two parties themselves as they enhance the clarity of some of the other details that have also not been totally completed.

Objection Six

"The architects of Geneva have assured the Israeli public that the Palestinian participants have renounced the demand for the return of refugees to pre-1967 Israel. There is no explicit renunciation of the Right of Return. So, while Israel is to tangibly repudiate its claim to Greater Israel by removing settlements, the Palestinians under Geneva aren't even obliged to verbally renounce their claim to Greater Palestine.... The Accord cites both the Saudi peace plan for the Middle East and UN resolution 194, both of which say that refugees should return to Israel. So, while the Accord does recognize 'the right of the Jewish people to statehood' (without saying that Israel is the fulfillment of that right), that concession is effectively nullified by the implicit endorsement of the Right of Return, which would make Jewish statehood untenable."

Response

I will deal with the Right of Return issue in the chapter addressing criticisms from the Palestinian Left. Here it is sufficient to say that most of them read the Accord in precisely the opposite way—attacking the Geneva Accord for failing to preserve the Right of Return. A more precise reading would acknowledge the concerns on both sides of the issue. On the one hand, the Geneva Accord does not explicitly say the words, "we, the Palestinian people, in signing this Accord, renounce forever our desire to return to the place where we were born." In that sense, the objection

raised by the Right is partially correct. And to help the Palestinian negotiators sell the Geneva Accord to their own people, it includes references to UN 194 which does call for a
return to Israel. On the other hand, the number of actual
people affected by any "return" is solely in the hands of the
Israeli people. The number of Palestinians to relocate in
their indigenous homeland within Israel is to be decided by
the sovereign decision of the State of Israel, and nothing in
the agreement forces the Israelis to accept back any greater
number than they choose. In public discussions, Yossi Beilin
has put forward a possible figure of 30,000 people who might
be allowed back to Israel. Only those on the Israeli side who
are determined to prevent any deal between the two sides
could possibly object to terms which are clearly favorable
to Israel and constitute none of the threats to Israeli sovereignty that are being claimed.

Objection Seven

"Under Geneva, no Jew could remain in the Palestinian state,
but Palestinians could live in both Israel and Palestine."

Response

There is no provision prohibiting Jews from living in the
Palestinian state. It is only the current settlers who would
be mostly moved, though some estimates are that approxi-

mately 100,000 would remain in their settlements which would then become part of Israel (in exchange for equal amounts of land given to Palestine). If Jews wanted to buy land in Palestine after this Accord goes into effect, nothing in the agreement itself prohibits that from happening. Similarly, if Jews wish to live in Palestinian cities, nothing in the Accord prohibits that from happening. Of course, nothing in the Accord prohibits either Israel or Palestine from sponsoring *de facto* conditions of discrimination or segregation as currently exist in Israel and so-called "Greater Israel" toward Arabs. For example, homes in settlements which have been built in the West Bank and Gaza are not open to Palestinians for purchase. But my main point here is that the Accord does not enforce this discrimination as suggested by the objection above.

Objection Eight

Palestinian refugees would be compensated, but the even larger numbers of Jewish refugees from Arab countries aren't even mentioned.

Response

I believe that this is a legitimate complaint about the Geneva Accord and that it ought to be rectified. Hundreds of thousands of Jews fled Arab lands in the period 1948–1967 based on well-founded fears of immediate danger. They ought to receive compensation for their losses and for their refugee-hood.

Objection Nine

The Geneva Accord "concessions" effectively "negate America's efforts to prove that terrorism doesn't work and to democratize the region. Under Geneva, the Palestinians would win immeasurable gains from their terrorism campaign. And, at a time when American forces are arresting terrorists around the world, thousands of Palestinian terrorists would be released from Israeli jails."

Response

If the English had used this argument to explain why they could never leave Palestine ("since doing so would reward terrorism"), the Jewish people would have rightly scoffed. Terrorists like Menachem Begin and Yitzhak Shamir went on to become prime ministers of the Jewish state. Similarly, until an agreement was reached to end apartheid, this same kind of reasoning was used to remonstrate against dealing with Nelson Mandela who headed an organization that was at times terrorist and did little to control the ongoing terror that continued through the elections even after apartheid had been officially dismantled. Indeed, from the standpoint of the English, the U.S. revolutionaries were terrorists and the same logic should have applied. When a country is prepared to yield its hold over another people who do not wish to be ruled, the country ceding power gives back to those who fought a national liberation struggle the right to enforce its own laws. End of discussion.

Objection Ten

"The Accord undercuts democratic norms in the only country in the Middle East that upholds them. The Sharon government was elected in a landslide victory to pursue a policy fundamentally incompatible with Geneva. The losers of that election are now trying to circumvent the electoral process and, together with the PA, impose their will by summoning international pressure for the Accord in order to delegitimize the Sharon government."

Response

What norms? What democracy for all? The peace movement and all who have sought to protect civil liberties and human rights are in fact interested in developing constraints on the "democratic norms" of Israeli society in the same way that the Bill of Rights, the U.S. Supreme Court, new laws, and amendments to the U.S. Constitution have attempted to do with regard to unrealized democratic norms in the United States. That has been the agenda of the U.S. civil rights movement, the women's movement, the labor movement, and other social-change movements: to use non-electoral forms of mobilization and pressure (including civil disobedience) to achieve ends that could not be reached solely through the ballot box. Social rebellion is part of the culture of American democracy.

On the other hand, it is preposterous to call Israel a society that upholds democratic norms when it prohibits several million of the people under its *de facto* control to participate in the democratic decision-making. Nor is this an emergency withholding of the right to vote under circumstances of insurrection. After Israel conquered the West Bank and Gaza there was a period of twenty-one years in which the population was largely quiescent, and yet Israel made no attempt to allow Palestinians the basic requisite of a democratic society: one person, one vote. Until Israel does so, it makes little sense to argue that exerting pressure from within or without is undermining democratic norms.

Objection Eleven

What about the Road Map presented by President Bush—shouldn't we just be supporting that?

Response

The Road Map (see above) is severely flawed. It asks the parties to take a series of steps that both sides will find difficult to initiate, yet it provides no clear vision of what the final outcome will be. Instead, at the end of the road map is not a destination, but a negotiation about what the destination should be. The Road Map does not empower moderates in the Palestinian world. When Arabs approach extremists to "stop the violence," they have nothing very convincing or enticing to offer. Conversely, Israeli moderates are unable to say to their own population, "If we give up some settlements now, we will get the following in the long run."

A second major flaw of the Road Map put forward by President Bush, the UN, Russia, and Europe is that it conditions steps toward peace on the elimination of all violence. Yet this gives a tremendous tool of empowerment and sabotage to the extremists who wish to stop the peace process—all they need to do is to get a few suicide bombers in place, and the whole thing gets derailed.

The Road Map would be valuable if it were explicitly linked to the Geneva Accord, so that it was the Road Map to implementing that Accord and if it were made one hundred percent clear that no acts of terror would be allowed to disrupt the process.

Objection Twelve

Why should people in the rest of the world have any right to shape what happens in Israel/Palestine? Isn't this a violation of their sovereignty?

Response

Israel was created by a vote of the United Nations, and as an act of affirmative action which imposed on the Palestinian people a refuge for world Jewry with a principle of Right of Return for Jews that was not granted to non-Jews. Creating Israel as a state for a particular ethnic/religious group, the UN participated in establishing and legitimizing a situation which has led initially to the dispossession of hundreds of thousands of Palestinians. Their families, now numbering over three million people, live in some of the worst conditions on this planet. The peoples of the world have a right and obligation to rectify the unjust consequences of their previous acts by now instituting a Palestinian state that encompasses almost all of the West Bank and Gaza.

5. Objections to the Geneva Accord from those who think it unfairly favors Israel

Objection One

The Geneva Accord does not represent the actual will of the Palestinian people, but only the position of those in the Palestinian Authority who are desperate for an end to the conflict with Israel. It actually involves selling out the long-term interests of the Palestinian people for the sake of some immediate gains. The Accord allows Israel to keep many of its settlements, albeit those that are in geographical proximity to the pre-1967 war Green Line, so that most of the current settlers will remain in the West Bank. It does not give the Palestinians what they have demanded all along— a return to the pre-67 Israel. The Accord merely reflects the current lack of power of the Palestinian people and must therefore necessarily be one-sided in giving to Israel more than it gives to the Palestinian people.

Response

It is true that the Accord will not push Israel back to the pre-67 Green Line, but it will give the Palestinian people a viable Palestinian state in approximately ninety-four percent of the West Bank, plus it will give the Palestinian state

an equivalent amount of land to make up for the six percent of the West Bank being given to Israel (and unlike the
proposed swap at Camp David, this land will not be in the
desert, but good quality farm land that would extend the
size of the Gaza strip).

The Accord represents major concessions on the part of
both peoples for the sake of achieving a lasting solution and
an end to the conflict. It does not merely repeat the current
power situation—which is so lopsided in favor of Israel that
its current government feels confident in its design to maintain control over far more than the Geneva Accord would
offer Israel. To talk of this proposal as a ratification of the
status quo is to miss the actual concessions being made by
Israel: giving up sovereignty over East Jerusalem (despite
decades of posturing that Jerusalem is "the united and eternal capital of the Jewish people"), giving up many of its
populous settlements, giving up control over the Temple
Mount, empowering an international force to provide protection for the Palestinian people, and participating in a fund
to pay compensation to Palestinian refugees.

As we saw in the previous section, many Israelis believe
that it is they who are giving up far too much. The reality
is that both sides are making significant compromises, and
only those seeking to make rhetorical points on behalf of
the notion that their side is more the "victim" can claim

that this agreement offers nothing to their side.

On the other hand, it is certainly true that the Accord does reflect the power imbalance. If the Palestinians had the superior army and were occupying all of Israel, it is unlikely that an Accord would follow the same boundaries that are currently being proposed. That is always the nature of agreements made to end war: they reflect who has the superior power.

What's the alternative? Perhaps it is to wait until the power balance has changed? That is a perspective that has far more appeal to those Palestinians and lefties living outside Palestine than those living under Occupation. For those living in the U.S. or France, waiting another fifty or a hundred years for the political power balance to change seems a plausible perspective. But for those living under Occupation, the desire to end the oppression is more immediate and pressing. After all, this is their life and the life of their children. No one knows what the world will be like in a hundred years. It's a fatuous gamble.

I personally sympathize with those who wish to end the oppression now, but I understand the logic of those who wish to wait till the power balance is different. And this question really underlies all the subsequent conversation of objections from the Left. If you are in no rush to end the conflict, as many lefties living in Europe or the United States are not, the Geneva Accord looks less appealing and its many concessions seem unprincipled and unnecessary. If, on the other hand, you are unwilling to allow the suffering of the Palestinian people to continue for another few generations, you may feel less moved by the objections being presented by those who are willing to wait until Israel's power declines considerably—an outcome that may not happen soon (or ever). Nor is it an outcome I'd particularly want to see happen, because I'm not sure that the Palestinians who were in power in such a moment would be any more generous to the Israelis than the Sharon government is to the Palestinians. So instead of waiting for yet another unfair configuration of power, I'd prefer to accept compromises that both sides can live with such as those articulated in the Geneva Accord.

Objection Two

The Geneva Accord acknowledges Israel as a Jewish state and thereby gives official sanction to the dominance of one religious group and one national entity, thus legitimizing discrimination against other religious and national groups within its borders.

Response

Israel does not need the Geneva Accord to function as a Jewish state. It was created by the United Nations as an act of affirmative action for a people who had been the subject of unparalleled oppression and genocide, and the majority of its people intend to keep Israel as a state that gives unique rights to its Jewish citizens—for example the special Right of Return that allows Jews to immigrate to Israel from anywhere in the world.

It will continue to be a Jewish state whether or not the Geneva Accord is adopted.

It is not particularly unusual for a state to function as the state of a particular people and to privilege its culture and history. Consider societies like France, Germany, Russia, or England. Each gives special attention to the history and culture of its dominant ethnic group. Like Israel, these societies grant equal rights to all of their citizens but, when it comes to shaping the culture of the society, they give special attention to the dominant ethnic group's proclivities and cultural choices.

You may then argue: "That's not true. There is discrimination against Israeli Arabs in Israel, and there are no rights given to West Bank Palestinians."

It is true that there is discrimination against minority

groups (though as foreign workers in Israel will tell you, this is not restricted to Arabs or Muslims). But there is also discrimination against minority groups in most other countries in the world. However, in Israel as in other countries, the discrimination is *de facto* and not *de jure,* except with regard to issues concerning immigration and serving in the Army. As to the lack of rights of West Bank Palestinians, the Geneva Accord is the way to rectify that.

"But Israel is a Jewish society, based on domination of one religion."

Yes, that is true, and I personally oppose this, as do many Israelis. However, there is nothing unusual about such societies in the Middle East. Syria, Egypt, Saudi Arabia, Iran, and Kuwait are a few other societies where religion plays the dominant role. As a rabbi, I believe that religious coercion by the orthodox establishment in Israel fosters so much resentment from secular Jews that it becomes the main obstacle to Jews being open to the wisdom and beauty of Judaism. Calls to end the special power of the religious in Israeli society should be supported. They would certainly receive a more receptive hearing in Israel were they part of a movement to de-Islamicize surrounding Islamic societies as well.

Objection Three

It is too late for a two-state solution—Israel has taken over too much of Palestinian land and is too deeply integrated into the West Bank. A two-state solution will never happen because Israelis will never be willing to voluntarily give up their control. So Israel ought to become a binational state composed of both Israelis and Palestinians sharing equal rights and jointly governing the entire area of pre-1948 Palestine.

Response

This is an idea that sings to the hearts of Western lefties, but has little resonance with the Palestinian people themselves or with the Israelis. To reject or downplay the possibilities created by the Geneva Accord for the sake of a solution that very few of the people on either side of this struggle actually wish for is to betray the survival needs of the Palestinian people and their expressed need for a state of their own; it is to ignore the historical experience of the Jewish people and their expressed need for a state of their own. Every time either of these peoples are asked what they want, they say they want their own separate states.

The idea of a binational state was first proposed by a group of progressive Zionists that gathered around Martin

Buber in the 1920s. Had it become the dominant perspective of the Zionist movement, it would likely have led to actions seeking to build bridges of understanding, cultural integration, and religious tolerance between Jews and Muslims. However, there was little resonance for this idea among most Jews who, within both Christian and Islamic societies, had had a long and bad experience of being a minority (which is what they would have been at that time, and what they believe, projecting current demographic trends, they would likely be again a few decades after a binational state came into existence). There was also little advocacy for this idea among Muslims, so it is reasonable to ask whether the binationalist alternative would have had serious support by Muslims unless they could ensure through restrictive immigration policies that Jews would remain the minority group.

Yet the idea of binationalism might eventually gain a foothold among Palestinians in the twenty-first century and their supporters around the world should the Occupation continue in some form. For example, if the Israeli government seeks to impose a solution on the Palestinians (either through negotiations or through unilateral moves) that would involve incorporating into Israel significantly more territory than the Geneva Accord allows, and then insists that the Palestinian people create a state on a tiny sliver of land that would make their state politically and economically unviable, it is conceivable that we could see Palestinians demanding to be incorporated into Israel and given the right of "one man, one vote." Indeed, if this were the demand of the Palestinian people, it would receive considerable support around the world from other peoples who have similarly struggled for democratic rights.

In my estimation, however, Israel would not accede to such a demand even if it had the support of most of the world's peoples. The Jewish people have been severely traumatized by the indifference of the world to their fate, an indifference which culminated in the Holocaust and in the closing of many of the gates of immigration to Jews. That trauma is restimulated whenever Jews find themselves facing unfair criticisms (for example, singling Israel out for castigations that should be given with equal or greater intensity to other countries). Furthermore, the recent revival of focus on the Jewish role in the crucifixion, traditionally the source of fresh waves of anti-Semitic attacks on Jews, through Mel Gibson's movie *The Passion of the Christ* reminds Jews that the world still tells terrible and unfair stories about them and hence that they need a place of refuge (which they could not be guaranteed of having should the dynamics of a binational state lead to the demographic triumph of those who want to abrogate a Jewish Right of Return).

Objection Four

Doesn't the Geneva Accord represent a strategy of political compromise contrary to our ideals? Shouldn't we fight against accommodation and for what we believe in? Isn't a binational, secular state the most honest and fair solution? Shouldn't we be part of a world transformation from religious to humane secular states?

Response

Yes and no. The Geneva Accord is imperfect in ways that I'll explore in the next chapter. For that reason, I advocate not uncritical but critical support for the Geneva Accord— along with exploration of other related strategies (see below).

Nevertheless, as long as we're talking about ideals, the higher ideal for which I'd want to struggle is not a binational state, but the elimination of states altogether and their replacement by bio-regional governing units that are designed specifically to address the major survival problem facing the planet today: the overcoming of the damage done to the Earth by 150 years of ecological irresponsibility by both capitalist and allegedly socialist societies.

If the social vision we wish to develop is long-range and utopian, we ought to be talking about transcending nation states, not figuring out how to build a new one with two nations contending within it for dominance. That is, since the two-state solution has no constituency today and would require decades of education before it could win support, why not save that kind of long-term reeducation for a much more visionary alternative—the elimination of Western states and their replacement by a global environmental solidarity that coordinates and shapes economic production and reduces pollutants in soil, water, and air. This may sound extreme at present, but, if planetary and species survival is at stake, its judiciousness may dwarf all sectarian conflicts.

Even if we are just talking about a way to end the oppression of the Palestinian people in the next twenty years (and at the same time maintain our ideals), a binational state is still a virtual impossibility, whereas the adoption and implementation of the Geneva Accord is not.

Still, the larger objection is partly valid. If we really want a world in which nation states have been transcended, if we really want environmental necessities to dictate a new way to organize our political life in order to reverse market trends that may lead to global disaster, then why shouldn't we focus on that as an immediate goal?

The answer is, we should. But we should also recognize that that goal may take twenty to thirty years (at least) to achieve, and that in the meantime there is the daily suffering of the Palestinian people, which could be alleviated by the creation of a viable Palestinian state along the lines defined by the Geneva Accord.

In the global campaign that should take place to transcend nation states and innovate global economic and political arrangements shaped by environmental survival needs, I would hope that Israel would be among the first twenty percent of all nations to agree to transcend national boundaries and become part of an emerging new world system. However, I don't expect Israel to have to be the first in line. Given the historical experience of the Jewish people, it might reasonably want to take its place in this process after this has been accomplished by the United States, France, Germany, England, Italy, Spain, Poland, Russia, Ukraine, China, Japan, Korea, Indonesia, India, Pakistan, Iraq, Iran, Saudi Arabia, Syria, Egypt, Argentina, Chile, Brazil, and Mexico. At that point, I'd want Israel to join this group.

If we can eventually create global political/economic units that are shaped by the need for global environmental sanity, I imagine that the one encompassing the Middle East will certainly be multinational, and that Jews would retain their cultural identity and religious institutions as a group within that larger unit, as would other ethnic, national, and religious communities. Once we have a world that is free of anti-Semitism, and Jews can live without fear of attack by others, I see every reason to encourage Jews to give up all remnants of nineteenth-century nationalism and return to their holy mission as one of the many spiritual witnesses to the possibilities of a world healed and transformed.

Objection Five

The Geneva Accord seems to make sense to people who have given up on changing Israeli policy in some other way. The peace forces in the world have never seriously attempted to use economic boycotts, disinvestment, cutting off aid to Israel, and the political muscle that it might have to pressure Israel to withdraw from the West Bank and give up its notion of itself as a strictly Jewish state. The Left ought to be using its time to mobilize this kind of disinvestment and anti-apartheid campaign against the Occupation, rather than capitulate to the ungenerous terms of the Geneva Accord.

Response

Attempts to analogize Israel to South Africa and imagine an anti-apartheid struggle succeeding against Israel are deeply misleading.

First, on the substance. Arabs living inside Israel are not denied the vote, but instead have representatives in the Israeli parliament (Knesset) and have the same rights as Jewish citizens to live anywhere, go to any beach or theater, sit on any bus, or use any public accommodations. The rights of

Palestinians in the Occupied Territories are being denied, but that denial is a political denial, not a racial one (because if they lived inside Israel, they'd have equal rights, though *de facto* they would still experience discrimination—as African Americans find in American society even while there are equal legal rights).

Because this is a political rather than a racial or religious denial of rights, and given the anger that many Americans feel at Palestinians when they see footage of Israeli civilians being blown to bits by Palestinian terrorists, there is little chance that any anti-apartheid boycott of Israel would have much support in the U.S. and hence it is unlikely to have much economic impact.

Similarly, the idea of cutting aid has attracted support among lefties who want to strike a blow against the Occupation. Cutting aid plays into the sympathies of many non-ideological Americans that we shouldn't be spending money supporting regimes abroad when we have not provided basic services for many people in the United States (an argument that I find misguided, because it seems to counterpose national needs against global ones).

The fundamental problem with these approaches is that they conceive Israel succumbing to external pressure brought by those who wish to label it "wrong." In this, they misunderstand the dynamics of Israeli society. Israel is filled with men and women who feel *they* have in fact been wronged by the peoples of the world. They are not willing to have their history misread in a one-sided way that makes them wrong. So, if faced with this kind of external assault, most Israelis, including many who support the peace movement, would rally to defend their country against external economic and political coercion. A campaign of this sort would dramatically weaken the peace forces inside Israel and would correspondingly strengthen the hawks and the Massada Complex. (The Massada Complex defines that tendency among Jews who have survived the previous destruction of the Jewish people to prefer to go down fighting even in a suicidal struggle than to give up. Israel has at its disposal an estimated eighty nuclear weapons. If faced with an economic and political assault waged by those who have no sympathy for Israel's side of the story, it is not inconceivable that Israelis would prefer to fight than to switch. The result could be a cataclysmic struggle in which hundreds of millions of people lost their lives).

I don't want to see the world facing that possibility. But the way to avoid it is to stop thinking of schemes to put Israel's back against the wall and force it to do something that would be impossible for it (namely, to end its existence as a Jewish state).

And there is an alternative strategy. That strategy is to

present Israel with an alternative that does not require the end of the Jewish state but does allow for the creation of a viable Palestinian state. That is precisely what the Geneva Accord provides.

If we are talking about putting new pressure on Israel to accept the Geneva Accord, then much of the past arguments fall away. A significant part of the Israeli population already supports the Accord. Perhaps political and economic pressure that was not directed against Israel in general, but only at the Occupation, and that was explicitly linked to an alternative to the Occupation, could be effective. But to be effective, it would have to be presented in a way that was sensitive to the history and experience of the Jewish people and was disentangled from the kind of anti-Israel rhetoric that has discredited much of the Left in the eyes of the Jewish people.

Objection Six

The Geneva Accord forces the Palestinian people to give up the Right of Return, thus abandoning the rights of refugees who constitute the bulk of the Palestinian people. Though that right may not be winnable in the short run, the Accord trades some paltry Israeli concessions for a fundamental right that has been given in the United Nations Declaration of Human Rights and which no negotiators have the authority or justification to abdicate.

Response

There are two different points here that need consideration: what does the Accord give up and what is the legitimacy of a Palestinian Right of Return?

As we saw in the objections from the Right, it is arguable whether or not the Palestinians have surrendered their "Right" to return should they sign the Geneva Accord. In this sense, the Accord may intentionally be leaving vague something as metaphysical as the status of a "right." It is not vague but clear in saying that the Palestinian people accept this as the final adjudication of claims based on their right, and so the Israelis would reasonably argue that the Palestinians are precluded by this agreement from insisting that they have a fundamental right to return to their homes beyond the terms offered in the Geneva Accord once this agreement was signed and implemented.

So is this fair?

To begin with, let's talk about the status of a Right of Return to one's homeland and one's home. There are several problems with this alleged right:

Is this "Right" time-limited and why should it be? If it is not time-limited, the Jewish people have a reasonable claim to return to their ancient homeland from which they were evicted by Roman imperialism and by the various successors to the Romans, including the military forces of Islam which conquered the area in the ninth and tenth centuries. The reality is that most lands in the world have been conquered by one group of humans after another and that it is hard to make any firm historical claims about who is the "original" group with a "right" to any land or any claim with regard to a specific territory that it is really someone's unique and exclusive homeland and not that of someone else.

Jewish tradition implicitly deals with this dilemma by acknowledging the actuality of some people owning land and, through the existing political system, however it has been established (and usually it has been established through force and violence originally), having a right to own and dispose of that land. However, it insists that, at the deepest level, the land belongs to God and that therefore people have to use land in a morally responsible way. In particular, the Land of Israel is said to be "holy" land, and that therefore it will "vomit out" its inhabitants should they act in immoral ways. The Torah makes clear that the moral way to behave with regard to land includes sharing its produce with the poor and with "the stranger" (in contemporary language, we could more appropriately label this "the other"— whoever that might be at a given moment) as well as letting the land lie fallow so that it can restore its nutrients once every seven years and (remarkably enough) redistributing the land every fifty years in such a way that all the inhabitants have roughly equal shares. (This, by the way, is the Torah law of the Jubilee—something I'm still hoping to see the religious fundamentalists of Judaism and Christianity implement with the same determination that they seek to implement other parts of Torah law).

No, I'm not expecting you, dear reader, to adopt Torah law. But I do want to highly commend to your attention the underlying idea here: that the land is God's and should be harvested and shared in a generous spirit. That is the mantra that should have remained central to both the early Zionist movement and to the Palestinian natives, and had it, we'd be in a very different circumstance today. But today is not too late to start to listen to sacred law.

And that's what the Geneva Accord does: it attempts to share the land.

"Wait a second," a Palestinian might object, "I don't want just any old part of the land, I want MY land back, the place where my grandfather tilled the soil and where my great-great-grandfather built a house. It's that particular land to which I am attached."

To see whether this is in fact a reasonable demand, let's consider another situation that may be less charged with emotional and religious baggage. In many American cities in the 1950s, '60s, and '70s, major sections of the inner cities underwent "urban renewal"; it frequently required tearing down buildings in which poor people, usually African Americans, had been living for generations, decimating neighborhoods in which they had built vibrant communities. The State then proceeded to rebuild those areas, often encouraging development of middle- and high-income apartments and condominiums that in turn were sold to people on the open market.

Imagine that you had worked for twenty or thirty years until you could afford to buy one such apartment in a building containing a hundred such apartments. Now, one day you get a knock on your door and find standing before you someone who says that s/he used to live at this very place in a slum building that was torn down. S/he further insists on her/his Right of Return and demands that you vacate the place. Or, even worse, dozens of families show up with the same demand, asking the hundred families who live there to move out.

It seems plausible that your response might be something like this: "I worked hard to buy this apartment, and I had nothing to do with the decision (made before I was born) to expel you and your family from the slum that used to be here. I don't live in that slum but in another building that wasn't even here at the time, and so do another hundred families. We regret what happened to you and do think that the State ought to provide you with some compensation for your loss. But don't expect to come back to this very spot where you lived, because doing so would be unfair to me who lives here now."

I hope this shows you why a "right of return" to the very spot you used to live could not be a real right at all.

So what we would plausibly ask of the State is that they give compensation to the people who got displaced, compensation sufficient so that they could find housing of comparable or superior quality to what they lost, and in a context where they could plausibly rebuild their community. But if the people who had been displaced started to demonstrate, or place bombs in the buildings where you lived and demanded their homes back, you'd probably elect to call the police rather than just to move out and hand them over your apartment. Or maybe not—maybe you'd agree to move, but that would be out of your own spirit of generosity, not because of a right that they had to get you to vamoose.

Once we start talking about compensation and recreating a community comparable to the one people once had, we are no longer talking about a "right of return," but rather about some way of making things right for those who had been dispossessed in a way that doesn't involve creating new injustices. I suppose on this logic, by the way, that had the Arab peoples of the Middle East said to the early Zionist movement: "We can't give you a place for a Jewish society in Palestine, but we can give it to you in Jordan or Lebanon or Syria," that they would have been in a far stronger moral position, and Jews probably should have accepted such an offer. Nothing of the sort was offered, however. But what is being offered to the Palestinian people is a substantial part of their own homeland back as a Palestinian state in the West Bank and Gaza, along with significant monetary compensation.

Monetary compensation must be adequate and fair. In my view, the formula should be something like this: take the median income of Israeli society today and use that as a standard for what should be offered to refugees. Then, adopt a set of steps necessary to provide that to the Palestinian people so that they are in that position within ten years of the time that the Geneva Accord is implemented. Those steps might include significant development in infrastructure, schools, health care, housing, and opportunities for employment. They would also include supplemental incomes for those living below the economic level of the median average of Israeli society today. In my view, this economic package of compensations should be offered both to Palestinians and to Jews who fled Arab lands from 1948–1967.

There is, however, another level of dealing with the Right of Return that I shall deal with in the next chapter—namely the spirit of the deal and how it is offered. While Palestinians should not have the right to show up and evict people from homes that they got from the Israeli government, they should be able to come to visit the places where these homes stood or still stand, the lands that they once tilled, the neighborhoods in which they used to live. They should be given time and opportunity to grieve over that which was lost and to get to know those who now live there. This simple human recognition of the pain of loss might go a long way toward making it possible for Palestinians to accept what is in fact incontrovertible: there is no way that those who once lived in these places are ever going to get back their land or their homes. "Get over it" is a harsh way of stating a deep truth: the desire to go back, however heartfelt and morally legitimate, is reasonable and yet unfulfillable. The Black poor will never be able to throw the middle class apartment dwellers out of their high-rises, and the Palestinian refugees who dream of returning to their land or homes are never going to succeed in driving out those who live there now— at least not without genocidal wars that would be no more justified than was the original expulsion of Palestinians.

Given this analysis, I believe it is the height of moral irresponsibility for Palestinian leaders or their cheerleaders in the West to continue to insist on a Right of Return. Doing so inflames desires that cannot and will not be fulfilled, while preventing people from acting on their own rational self-interest so that they might achieve what is in fact achievable: the creation of a two-state solution as detailed in the Geneva Accord.

Does that mean that Palestinians must give up the dream of return? No. Religious Jews can continue to dream of the rebuilding of the Temple on the Temple Mount and the restoring of the sacrificial services that are enjoined in Torah and for which they have prayed for the past two thousand years, as long as that doesn't lead them to reject the Geneva Accord (or an equivalent agreement) or lead them to take actions to try to physically or politically grab hold of the Temple Mount. Palestinians likewise have the right to continue to dream of a return to their homes and their land, as long as that doesn't interfere with them accepting the actual benefits and responsibilities of a Geneva Accord and the daily reality of building peaceful relationships on its basis. The Palestinian people can continue to write songs and poems and short stories about return, just as Jews can envision a return to the Temple Mount or even to their former homes in the West Bank or in Hebron. Any fantasy is allowed and may even serve some useful psychic purposes— as long as people know the difference between fantasy and reality and do not make political decisions based on believing that the fantasy can come true if only they struggle longer or harder and more uncompromisingly.

When the Right of Return is used as an argument against accepting something that is actually possible to achieve in the next two years—a real Palestinian state with significant compensation for refugees—it becomes an enemy to peace and an enemy to the best interests of the Palestinian people. Dreams and real possibilities are not the same currency and should not be offered in place of each other.

Having said all that, I do want to distinguish very strongly between a "Right" of return—with all its coercive implications that someone is unfairly depriving you of a right and hence that they are acting unfairly and you should use whatever power you can to help you restore your rights—and the fact of return. The "Right" of return is an ideological grenade, an automatic nonstarter. I do, however, believe that there can be *de facto* return of many Palestinians to the general vicinities of where they used to live.

How, then, will that happen?

There is nothing in the Geneva Accord which precludes a future Israeli society from deciding that the number of Palestinians it wishes to bring back is not, as Yossi Beilin suggests, somewhere around 30,000, but rather that is 300,000 or 500,000 or more. As long as the decision is made totally by the sovereign right of the Israeli people and not under coercion or demand, that could conceivably happen within the next twenty to fifty years.

What will make that happen is the ironically only one thing: unequivocal renunciation of the Right of Return on the part of the Palestinian people so that Israelis no longer feel that they are being coerced into something that they don't believe is legitimate. Full implementation of the Geneva Accord for a period of five to ten years in a way that gives the most moderate Israelis the sense of certainty that there is no longer anything to fear from the Palestinian people would make return less threatening.

Foreigners move into neighborhoods all the time. It's been that way from the Stone Age through the 'burbs. Election of a peace-oriented Israeli government that is committed to a new spirit of reconciliation might actually make Israeli sponsorship of some return a social program of the government. For those who think that is unlikely to the point of ludicrous, I would point them to South Africa and even Northern Ireland, where peace and accord have built their own esprit and momentum. There are rituals of redemption and renewal as well as rituals of war and destruction. I shall turn to that new spirit of reconciliation in the next chapter.

I believe that the Palestinian people and their allies abroad must make a fundamental choice: between asserting the Right of Return on the one hand, and actually achieving partial return for hundreds of thousands of Palestinians, on the other. As long as the "Right" is being insisted upon, the

Israeli people will feel under attack, the legitimacy of their state in question, and their most generous side will be subordinated to their most fearful side.

I believe that the real friends of the Palestinian people will tell them the truth—that a demand for a Right of Return is the opponent of their actually getting a limited but real return. It was this kind of "practical wisdom" that led the Zionist movement in 1947 to accept a partition agreement developed by the United Nations even though that agreement did not give the Jewish state any power over Jerusalem. The Palestinian people, on the other hand, rejected the agreement, though had they accepted it they would have been granted a state considerably bigger than the one that is now envisioned by the Geneva Accord. I truly hope that the Palestinian people will embrace the Geneva Accord now and join with the peace elements in Israel and around the world who are prepared to launch a campaign of support for Geneva or some comparably fair plan.

Not all moments are comparable. The Geneva Accord is on the table now, but it may be successfully sidelined by Ariel Sharon and his successors and become an unachievable goal in the future. So I am writing this book in hopes that this opportunity is not squandered by peace-desiring peoples on either side of this conflict.

6. What the Geneva Accord Lacks— and How it Can Be Repaired

Up until now in this book I've tried to show what is powerful in the Geneva Accord. A debt of thanks is due to Yossi Beilin* and Yasser Abed Rabbo for the work that they put into shaping this very impressive legal document and diplomatic agreement. I believe that, despite most of the objections to it, it is not seriously flawed.

There is, however, one huge problem that the Accord doesn't address and in fact couldn't possibly address: namely, how in the world is it ever going to be adopted as the policy and implemented?

Or to put it in another way: what could turn this from a dry set of formulas into a living reality that has the power to stir people to actually want to implement it?

My short answer is this: the Geneva Accord is not meant to be an inspiring document like the Declaration of Independence. What inspires about it is that it provides us with a way of imagining how things might practically work once

---

*Yossi Beilin was elected chair of the new political party Yachad (Hebrew word meaning: Together) in mid March, 2004. Yachad was built from the previous peace party Meretz, plus elements from the peace faction of the Labor Party.

people wanted to build peace. As a dose of sober reality, it is also a dose of hope.

What it lacks is the strategy to get people to the point at which they would want to make it work. That strategy can be supplied by a movement that is built around the Geneva Accord, though it must be a groundswell that goes far beyond the Accord to confront a set of spiritual, psychological, and historical issues that are not in the document itself but need to be addressed now by those who want to make the Accord something more than another failed attempt at peace.

The sensitivities and skills required are in short supply among those who normally engage in politics and diplomacy. That is why we need a movement to build a Middle Eastern peace that is quite different from the kinds of movements we have had heretofore, plying skills and ways of thinking that may not be uncommon in Jewish, Christian, and Muslim societies but *are* uncommon among those who, one way or another, have become their political activists and leaders. What is needed, then, is the involvement of people who are not normally involved in politics yet who wish to make a real contribution to healing our planet. That might be you, dear reader!

Warning to those who are normally allergic to spiritual or psychological discourse: don't you dare skip this part—because even if the language feels off-putting, its insights can be translated by you into a language that does not use explicitly spiritual terms and yet is extremely useful for political transformation.

Peace is not just a legal process—it is a spiritual process and requires not only formal agreements but a change in the consciousnesses of the people who would live in a peaceful world.

We can't get to peace without effecting transformations in consciousness on the part of those who have been locked into blind struggle. I believe that reading the Geneva Accord and visualizing how it might work is one part of that process, but there are other steps that are necessary, that speak to the spiritual needs of the combatants. I am not referring to the formal religions of the combatants, which have been mobilized repeatedly on behalf of one side or the other and which have played more destructive than positive roles (though, of course, that too is reversible).

1. A new spiritual consciousness.

Almost every tribe on the planet has elements of a shared spiritual tradition that underlies its specific religious beliefs. Although often marginalized and underplayed, these spiritual truths can be reclaimed on behalf of inner transformation and peace. Changes in consciousness can become changes on the ground. In fact, they are the best way to bring about lasting changes on the ground.

The most important spiritual insights are these: We are all One—that is, human beings are fundamentally interconnected, interdependent, and ontologically equally valuable. We are all children of the same God, however we chose to identify and name our God. The issues and categories that separate us have been given too much primacy, while the commonality and shared plight that unite us have been too minimized in contemporary Western culture. What we are learning today, as much from environmental science as from spiritual traditions, is that there is no secular solution to the problems we face—no imaginable fix—until we recognize that we are all in this together. That is the great lesson of the present global crisis.

Nothing could be more important for Jews, Christians, and Muslims to understand. Each group has developed ideas, religious practices, cultural identities, and mind-sets that reinforce their separateness. In that separated state people come to believe that their own group's survival and security depend upon its ability to dominate and control some "other." Spiritual insight teaches the opposite: that we need each other and need each other's well-being. In fact, each of us will do better, get more of what we need, if we can focus on making sure that others also get what they need.

2. There is enough: a spirituality of generosity and open-heartedness.

Most people, including almost everyone involved in the Middle East conflict, have the false belief that life is a zero-sum game, that the world doesn't have enough for us, and so we must struggle with others to get our needs met. It was this false premise that gave currency in the past to the notion that the Land of Israel could not be shared. Now we know that this is not true, that there is enough land for both Israelis and Palestinians—if it is shared in an ecologically sensitive and sustainable way and if the principle of sharing is extended to the rest of the world as well.

I've often been impressed when visiting both Israeli and Palestinian homes by how quickly the families involved open their hearts to strangers and share with them whatever they have. The spirit of generosity is already part of the culture of both Arabs and Jews—it only needs to be validated, liberated from constraints, and directed toward the "other."

When one is coming from a consciousness that there is enough and that generosity is a necessary value for one's own growth and happiness, it becomes much easier to approach the other with a spirit of open-heartedness.

And the spirit of open-heartedness is contagious. When people feel that they are being given to not as a manipulation (i.e., "giving to get") but from a shared humanity, a genuine expression of a desire for the well-being of the other, they typically respond in kind.

And that makes all the difference in the world. If there is a spirit of generosity in the way that we approach each other, distrust of the other can be dispelled and hope can be regenerated.

By contrast, consider the way that Oslo was implemented. Neither side felt that they could embrace the other and reach out with a spirit of generosity. Instead, they tried to show how "realistic" they were by maintaining an appearance of "cynical detachment" from the very peace process that they were seeking to validate. No enthusiasm means no real commitment. This doesn't work; it can't work. The parties to the conflict have dug too deep a hole to climb or think their way out of step by step, weighing each one for a possible booby-trap.

There are many people who embrace the Geneva Accord but who feel that in order to maintain their credibility among fellow Israelis (or Palestinians) they must maintain an aura of dispassionate distance and critical reserve. So instead of talking about a new spirit of hope and generosity and open-heartedness, they think they make themselves appear more credible by talking in narrow terms of self-interest.

I heard one of the "advocates" of the Geneva Accord

address an audience of Jews with his entire focus on the claim that the Accord would be the only way to ensure the Jewish character of Israel by making sure that it didn't have too many Arabs who could make a claim to citizenship. Geneva thus became a path to demographic security. Well, perhaps it is *also* that. But when that becomes the major incentive for why to support Geneva, the rationale elicits people's most cynical side—and when people are in that mode of thought, the counter-arguments about why not to trust "the other" take on more persuasiveness, so Geneva supporters implicitly feel on the defensive.

When the members of "the other side" (whether that be Israelis for some, Palestinians for others) hear that kind of discourse, their most paranoid concerns seem justified. They become less willing to trust because they've heard "the other side" talking in the cynical language of self-interest. The warnings of the critics begin to sound more persuasive than their own peace and reconciliation convictions, and so they tend toward wanting to take fewer actions of a generous sort themselves. Paranoia becomes self-fulfilling, as participants on both sides respond from the logic of fear and distrust of the other.

It is incredibly naïve to think that one can build peace while dodging the hard issues and personal changes needed for reducing distrust of the other. It is far more sophisticated and savvy to act from a standpoint of open-heartedness, knowing that in so doing one will touch the heart of the other. And it is touching of the heart of the other that is actually the most self-interested thing we can do. That is, the smart way to be self-interested is to consistently and through one's entire life act in a genuinely caring and open-hearted way.

We can build a new climate of hope— here are some concrete steps to take:

Do not let the fear and despair mongers convince you that changing consciousness is impossible. From the standpoint of the Jewish people, the steps to be taken to produce change might include actions like this:

a. Begin a far-reaching campaign to collect and deliver food and other necessary supplies to the Palestinian people currently living in refugee camps.

b. Send medical care and doctors to refugee camps. Create a "peace corps" of Jewish volunteers who attend to assist in any way possible to improve the quality of life of the Palestinian people living under Occupation. Come as proud members of the Jewish people—not as Jews who reject Jewishness, but as Jews who are expressing their commitment to their Jewishness through service to others.

c. Invite Arabs, Muslims, and Palestinians to your home.

Get to know them. Build family and individual friendships.

d. When saying Kaddish (the prayer of mourning for the dead) in synagogues, read the names of both Israelis and Palestinians who have been killed in the past week—and mourn for both.

e. Read the poetry and novels of Arab and particularly Palestinian writers. Learn their music and be open to experiencing their culture. Organize events that bring together Arabs and Jews for sharing cultural experiences.

f. Seek to have your local synagogue, Jewish community center, and Jewish Federation collect monies to help in rebuilding Palestinian homes that have been torn down in order to make way for the Wall of Separation being built by the Israeli government.

g. Stop the teaching of hatred toward Arabs and Muslims in general and Palestinians in particular, a propaganda that often accompanies the lessons to which Jewish children are exposed in their religious schools or Hebrew schools.

h. Insist that any official Jewish trip to Israel include an equal amount of time for visiting the leaders of Palestinian people who support the Geneva Accord. Bring home their stories to counter the frequently-asked rhetorical question: Where are the voices of peace and compromise in the Palestinian world?

i. Practice noticing the positive aspects of Palestinian culture—and then talk about them to others.

j. Whenever you hear of an incident in which Palestinian civilians have been killed by the Israeli army by mistake or as collateral damage while the IDF was seeking terrorists, send a letter of condolence to the families of those who were killed.

If you live in Israel, add the following:

k. Insist that your political leaders talk about the suffering of the Palestinian people and that the political parties to which you give support spend part of their time educating Israelis about this reality. Don't allow the peace forces to speak *only* about the way that peace will be in the interests of the Jews—insist that they *also* seek to foster a sense of the legitimacy of the fate of non-Jews in general and Palestinians in particular.

l. Speak and build from the religious and cultural history of the Jewish people—and make that an integral part of your discourse. Yes, it's true that parts of that religious and cultural history have gotten mired in chauvinism, insensitivity to the other, cruelty, and glorification of genocide. That is the case of every religious tradition, but also of every nonreligious tradition as well (compare, for example, the bloody history of those who used socialism as their excuse to murder tens of millions in Stalinist Russia or those who used making the world safe for democracy as their excuse to invade other countries and dominate people and cultures around the world). What's important to note is that there is a living marrow of Jewish tradition that is affirming of generosity, caring for others, peace, social justice, and kindness. Instead of suffering your own tradition to be appropriated by the political and religious right-wingers, reclaim the positive elements of that tradition. And on that foundation, approach Palestinians and affirm to them that aspect of Jewish identity, so that they don't get the impression that the only people who want peace in Israel are those who entirely reject or distance themselves from their Jewishness. Rather, act as Jews who embrace Jewish compassion and see that as the center of their identity and hence as the center of how they relate to non-Jews.

m. Don't allow your caring for the suffering of the Palestinian people to obscure your caring for the well-being of fellow Jews as well. Don't become so obsessed with what is wrong with the Occupation that you forget what is good and right about Israel and Israelis. Instead, convey to your fellow Israelis the conviction that your open-heartedness toward Palestinians is totally consistent with open-heartedness toward fellow Israelis. There are several actions that may help convey such a message: a. Insist that any peace party running for Knesset give equal attention to the social justice needs of the Israeli public, with special emphasis on the fate of Sephardi/Mizrachi Jews (those whose families fled from Arab lands), Ethiopian and Russian Jews, and non-Jewish immigrants. b. Hold memorial services for Israelis killed by acts of terror. Send letters of condolence to the victims of terror. Help in the rebuilding of places that have been assaulted by terror. c. Help West Bank settlers resettle inside the Green Line.

I don't have a similarly worked-out list for Muslims or Arabs or Palestinians because I am not equally familiar with the details of how those communities operate. Moreover, given the unequal power balance at the moment and the reality that many Arabs feel acutely oppressed by the Jewish people, given the overwhelming support the Jewish people in the Diaspora appear to give to the current Israeli government, it is likely that Arab acts of open-heartedness will be more in response to Jewish ones than taking a vanguard role. However, I can think of a few simple steps:

a. Send letters of condolence to victims of terror. Attend or create public memorial ceremonies on behalf of the victims of terror attacks in Israel.

b. Make strong alliances with Jews who wish to build peace and begin reconciliation. Instead of focusing on points of disagreement, embrace the wide areas of agreement. Invite Jewish people to your homes and to your mosques and religious celebrations.

c. Read the poetry and fiction of Israeli writers and thinkers. Become familiar with Jewish history. Learn about the way that Jews were treated in Arab lands.

d. Challenge the teaching of hatred against Jews and Israelis that sometimes takes place in religious and secular schools, in the United States, Palestine, and throughout the Arab world.

e. Publicize the statements and activities of Jewish and Israeli peacemakers to and through the media and institutions of the Arab and Islamic worlds.

3. Acknowledgment, repentance, atonement.

The "progressive Middle Path" being fostered by the Tikkun Community insists that both sides have a legitimate story to tell and legitimate claims. I've presented these in greater detail in my book *Healing Israel/Palestine.* But we also insist that both sides have acted in ways that are insensitive to the other, cruel, and require recognition, remorse, penance, and redemption.

A discourse acknowledging that both sides need to make spiritual amends is critical to getting to the point where the Geneva Accord can be fully accepted and really implemented.

The termination of South African apartheid may have been dramatically catalyzed by the creation of a Truth and Reconciliation Commission. Each day, the hearings of this commission provided a forum for the "truths" that each side had sought to conceal: the full extent of the barbarity of apartheid and its enforcers, on the one hand, and on the other, the perversities that had been committed in the name of overthrowing apartheid by the African National Congress and its allied groups and individual members. Full disclosure has a powerful and healing impact on a society, particularly when accompanied by statements of genuine remorse.

The Israel/Palestine conflict may eventually require such a process. But that can only happen in a full way once the Geneva Accord itself is being implemented—there cannot be meaningful reconciliation as long as the Occupation persists.

What can take place now is the beginning of a real process of acknowledgement, repentance, and atonement on the part of those who will allow themselves to genuinely aspire to this kind of spiritual consciousness.

For example, it would be a powerful message if significant numbers of Jews and Christians used the period from Rosh Hashanah to Yom Kippur (usually in mid September) to focus on the actual acts of murder, human rights violations, and humiliations that had been delivered to the Palestinian people by the State of Israel and its agents in the West Bank and Gaza, and were then to publicly acknowledge these acts, repudiate them, and commit themselves to not giving any more support to those who perpetrate such deeds. This might be followed by acts in which the penitents bought advertising in Palestinian newspapers to ask for forgiveness for their parts in having allowed their own—Israeli or U.S.— government to carry out or be complicit in these activities.

An extension of this activity would be to arrange trips of Americans to Israel/Palestine, one of whose foci was to visit the homes of those who have been killed in both Israel and Palestine, to express sorrow and to convey commitment to peace. These kinds of person-to-person gestures of sadness and atonement could have a powerful impact in transforming hatred to reconciliation.

4. Transcending victimhood and acknowledging the history: Israel and Jews taking the first step.

The Geneva Accord requires Palestinians to give up the fantasy of a Right of Return. That will be very hard. But Israel needs to give up something as well: the fantasy of being an innocent victim of irrational Arab hatred. Of course, there has been plenty of irrational Arab hatred toward Jews— and that makes it all the harder to give up the fantasy part.

But it might help to remember that there was also plenty of provocation by Jews. In particular, recent historical research has disclosed that Jews played a particularly disturbing role in causing Arabs to flee their homes in the period between 1947–1949, and that became an initiating cause of the current struggle—not the only cause, and Jews don't have the only responsibility—but they have a major responsibility for co-creating the Palestinian refugee problem.

In light of the superior power that Israel currently wields over the Palestinian people, it would be an important act for Israel and the Jewish people to take the lead in offering acts of penitence and words of conciliation.

For example, the Jewish people could send statements to each and every refugee family asking to be forgiven. In the context of implementing the Geneva Accord, that kind of action would serve as testimony to a new spirit of contrition coming from the Jewish world.

The partisans from the Jewish world are likely to respond, "Yeah, I'll do that. Sure. The day hell freezes over! What about them and their acts of contrition? When will they apologize for their cowardly acts of terror?" And the answer, I'm afraid, is: "Not too soon." Why? Because in the current situation it is the Palestinians who are experiencing direct oppression and subordination, and from that standpoint, of being underneath, it is much harder to act in a spirit of magnanimity and contrition. Jewish people are going to have to walk this lonesome valley alone. And before you start screaming hysterically at me, think about the true courage, charity, and transformation of Judaism itself, as practiced in the present, that that will entail. A Jewish people who had the courage to acknowledge being wrong and hurtful toward Palestinians and resolved to building a spirit of public repentance would earn the respect of their own next generations, who may otherwise wish to distance themselves from a people still so frozen in their own trauma that they are unable to embody their own ideals. Open-heartedness and generosity are the key to Jewish survival and Jewish continuity. Or to put this in religious language, being an embodiment of God energy is the most realistic path for the Jewish people. That's why Jews should take the first step in this process of reconciliation and atonement.

On the other hand, while the power imbalance dictates who goes first, it does not obviate the Palestinian people from acts of repentance as well. In fact, as Jewish people and Israelis begin to take such actions in a public and consistent way, it will free the most generous and open-hearted Palestinians to take similar actions from their side. That will then generate its own momentum from there. Within a few decades it will be possible to have Palestinians talking openly about the immorality of the acts of terror against Israeli civilians and for them to make public stands of contrition as well. Not a fairy tale. The way the world has to work, if we want a place where we all can live.

So the task is not to slough all blame on one side or the other but to break through the frozen fears on both sides and to allow for a new spirit of generosity to flow back and forth. And that can be greatly aided by public acts of repentance on the part of Jews and Israelis to start a process that must eventually include both sides.

5. Nonviolence and recognizing the good in the oppressors.

There is no question that one mighty spiritual action that could dramatically change the dynamics of the Israel/Palestine struggle and facilitate almost instantaneous implementation of the Geneva Accord would be if the vast majority of the Palestinian people and their leadership were to explicitly repudiate Hamas, Islamic Jihad, and all acts of violence against Israel, and commit themselves to a totally nonviolent struggle.

Such a commitment, if held to and enforced in a serious way, would melt through the frozen and fearful hearts of many Jews and Israelis and would make possible a whole new spirit of generosity.

Let me be clear that by nonviolence I do not mean "less

violent" or "occasionally nonviolent." A demonstration in which rocks are thrown at troops is not nonviolent. I remember during Intifada I in 1988 that I was driving through Wadi Qelt in Jerusalem on my way to the Mt. Scopus campus of the Hebrew University when a group of Arab teenagers unleashed a salvo of rocks at my car that shattered my window and made me veer into what could have been a very dangerous crash. I always have trouble when others now tell me that the first Intifada was the good one because it was nonviolent. It was certainly less violent, but that is not what I mean when I say that a nonviolent movement would have a tremendous psychological impact on the Israeli population.

"Why should we Palestinians have to worry about the psychological well-being of the Israeli occupiers?" a Palestinian might ask me. I would respond: "Because you will be better off if Jews can come to believe that they will be safe once you have real power and a state of your own. It is not unusual for those who have found themselves in the position of oppressing some other group to imagine that should they lift their symbolic boot from the neck of the oppressed the oppressed will jump up and kill them. So for that reason, it makes sense for the oppressed to convince them that removing the boot will be safe—and that the credibility of the offer of truce originates from the fact that the oppressed recognize the fundamental humanity and decency of the oppressors first even if the oppressors are unable to recognize the decency and humanity of those whom they are oppressing."

"That's an outrageous demand," some Palestinians respond. "Why should we have to convince the oppressors, in this case Israelis and their Jewish and American supporters, that we see their humanity? They are the ones who are not seeing our humanity—so let them convince us first."

I agree with the reasonableness of that conviction on the part of the oppressed to have the oppressor "get over it" first. But unfortunately, I'm not optimistic that that can happen without there being simultaneous transformation in the way that the oppressed act toward the oppressors.

This is the brilliance of the nonviolent strategy of Martin Luther King, Jr. and Mahatma Gandhi and Nelson Mandela. Each of these leaders managed to overcome a far more powerful opponent by showing the oppressor that the oppressed recognized his humanity.

Consider the powerful example set by Martin Luther King, Jr. By the mid 1960s some African Americans had given up on white America and were talking about armed struggle to liberate the oppressed. The Black Panther Party and similar groups sought to arm Blacks for that struggle. But of course, the superior military strength of white society made it easy to defeat such struggles on the basis of sheer strength and armaments. Black Panther Party chapters were decimated by police who were able to use the excuse of the Panthers' militant rhetoric to justify violent assaults against them even when the Panthers were not actually involved in violent actions. Contrast that with Martin Luther King, Jr., whose nonviolent movement was accompanied by religious services (all of the marches started inside churches, then went outside), prayer, songs, and a discourse that validated the goodness of American whites. King's rhetoric was never hateful but always hopeful, never succumbing to stereotyping the white person as evil but ever affirming that they too had an equal place and a place of honor in the kind of world that King's movement hoped to build. It was this way of speaking that reassured whites that they would not be destroyed should they agree with the political demands of the civil rights movement.

"But you are suggesting that the oppressed should take responsibility for the mental state of the oppressors. The oppressed have enough problems. To ask that of us just is not fair and it's not right!"

Here we get to the central strategic issue with which people seeking peace and justice and social healing must grapple: would they prefer to be right or would they prefer to be smart? They are not the same thing. It isn't right to demand that the oppressed worry about and develop strategies to address the psychology of the oppressors—but it may be very wise to do that.

Being smart requires making demands on oneself or on one's group that may not be fair or right. But doing so may lead to a winning strategy.

Unfortunately, many people in the social change movements feel more comfortable losing but knowing that they are "right" than they would feel winning. I've analyzed these psychological dynamics in my book *Surplus Powerlessness* (Humanities Press, 1991). I show that one of the ways in which oppressed people internalize their experience of helplessness is to embrace it and feel that this is the right way to be, the way that is appropriate to them. As a result, they feel awkward, out of sorts, and inappropriate when they have the opportunity to win or be powerful. They will do everything they can to get back to their comfort zone where they can see themselves as powerless and undeserving of any significant victory. When they participate in political struggles that they win, they focus instead on all that is yet to be won, finding it impossible to celebrate the victories that they actually have achieved. And when they look at any new situation, they gravitate to ways of being that will make them feel comfortable. So they will debate theory endlessly rather than risk actually going out to talk to new people and to try to convince them of progressive ideas. Or they will expend their energies fighting against their own leaders, bad-mouthing their own spokespeople, and spreading gossip and negativity about each other. Or they will be attracted to strategies that have no chance of winning and hence do not put them in an awkward position of having to handle success.

This is a psychological disability of the powerless. And it can be remedied. One important step is for those of us who have a little less surplus powerlessness to not allow those with more of it to define our strategies for us. Rather, it is important to allow ourselves to take paths that might actually lead to winning. And in this context, that means strategies that would lead to genuine healing between Israel and Palestine.

One important element in combating surplus powerlessness is to challenge the morbid certainty that success is impossible and therefore not worth taking risks to achieve. A central task of Middle Eastern peacemakers in the early part of the twenty-first century is to replace that pessimism with a new attitude of hopefulness and to not allow that hopefulness to be dispelled by acts of stupidity or cruelty on the part of those on each side of this conflict who do not want a settlement that will give Israel real security and Palestinians a viable state. Our counter-strategy is to give more energy to the part in each of us that wants a world where love and kindness can replace domination and cruelty. That is the central spoke of a strategy for lasting peace.

When I talk this way, you can understand why I believe that you, dear reader, may be able to play a more significant role in this process than some of the most sophisticated political activists and diplomats. They have their valuable contributions to make, also. But too many of them will dismiss this way of thinking as soft, flaky, and adolescent— they've adopted the cynical realism of the media and their political opponents, thinking that that will make them more effective politically. Unfortunately, it is precisely that way of thinking that makes much more difficult the kind of jumps in consciousness that would bring about the victory of a peace process in the Middle East. That's why I'm addressing you and hoping that you have not yet have fallen into this trap, in which case you can make a very significant contribution to building peace.

What the Geneva Accord lacks is heart and soul energy. It's got a great head, lots of details, lots of well-crafted arrangements. What it needs now is a way to speak to the hearts and souls of Israelis, Palestinians, and Americans. And that is what we can do—we can begin an enterprise that is well-crafted to speak to this level of human reality. If we do, if we build a movement that is psychologically sophisticated, spiritually sensitive, and capable of speaking a language of the heart, we can use the foundation of the Geneva Accord to bring lasting peace and reconciliation to the Middle East.

What You Can Do!

1. Join one of the groups doing work to promote the Geneva Accord. They include:

- The Tikkun Community: www.Tikkun.org, 510-644-1200, Community@tikkun.org. An interfaith organization, working in the Jewish, Christian, Muslim, and Buddhist communities and among secular people, for peace and justice (not only in the Middle East, but globally on behalf of ecological restoration, human rights, and economic democracy). Chaired by Rabbi Michael Lerner, Tikkun integrates the spiritual politics delineated in this book. Chapters throughout the United States are involved in getting the Geneva Accord endorsed and discussed by policy makers and public-opinion shapers.

- Brit Tzedeck v'Shalom. Contact: "Aliza Becker" aliza @btvshalom.org. An organization of Jews for Israel/ Palestine peace with chapters around the U.S. primarily doing in-reach into the Jewish community.

- Americans for Peace Now: www.peacenow.org, apndc @peacenow.org. An organization that brings Israeli speakers to the U.S. to promote peace.

- Israel Policy Forum: www.IsraelPolicyForum.org. Israel Policy Forum: ipfdc@ipforumdc.org. An organization that provides information and analysis and sponsors a forum for policy makers.

2. Ask your local city council and other elected officials to publicly endorse the Geneva Accord.

3. Come to the yearly Teach-In for Middle East Peace in Washington, D.C. (we are creating a progressive alternative to AIPAC). Info: community@tikkun.org.

4. Make support for the Geneva Accord a condition for your support for any candidate running for Congress, U.S. Senate, or the presidency.

5. Regularly call media to insist that they present the perspective of the peace movement (info on how to do this: media@tikkun.org).

6. Volunteer at the Tikkun national office or from your home (members@tikkun.org) for phone calling and other outreach/educational work.

7. Create a study group around *Healing Israel/Palestine,* this book, and latest analyses in TIKKUN Magazine and become knowledgeable enough so that you can do public speaking about the latest developments. Call 510-644-1200 for help in getting started.

The Terra Nova Series

The Terra Nova Series comprises short texts by prominent twenty-first century authors exploring topics in the arts, cultural history, politics and international relations, and ethnic identity. The series is divided into:

American Narratives: Statements from the American experience addressing a global context; and

Global Perspectives: Texts by international writers addressing the boundaries and interplay among nations, peoples, ideologies, and cultural representations.

American Narratives

Brando Rides Alone
A Reconsideration of the Film *One-Eyed Jacks*
Barry Gifford
$10.95 paper, 1-55643-485-5, 112 pp.

The People's Democratic Platform
$10.95 paper, 1-55643-498-7, 80 pp.

Seven Pillars of Jewish Denial
Shekinah, Wagner, and the Politics of the Small
Kim Chernin
$11.95 paper, 1-55643-486-3, 112 pp.

Global Perspectives

Empire 2.0
A Modest Proposal for a United States of the West by Xavier de C***
Prologue by Régis DeBray
$11.95 paper, 1-55643-495-2, 144 pp.

www.northatlanticbooks.com